THE STORY OF THE MAN BEHIND THE NAME

GilbertOrtega

THE STORY OF THE MAN BEHIND THE NAME

as told to
Patricia Bezunartea

January 2007, Patricia Bezunartea

ⓖ Gilbert Ortega Family Publications
3925 N. Scottsdale Road
Scottsdale, Arizona 85251
480 / 990-1808
www.gilbertortegabook.com

Printed in the United States of America
by Biltmore Pro Print, Phoenix, Arizona

ISBN: 978-1-4243-0839-2

Editing: Deborah Hilcove, Marcia Sawyer
Cover Concept: Desirée Ortega

TABLE OF CONTENTS

Preface

For nearly a year, I spent almost every Sunday with Gilbert Ortega at his home, interviewing him, taping his stories and anecdotes, delving into deep discussions about business, talking about life.

On those Sundays, the only interruptions were calls from the sales people in his stores. He was always accessible, and he loved those phone calls. That meant that even though he wasn't at one of his stores, he was still linked to the business — the umbilical cord was never cut.

His sprawling Paradise Valley home was an opulent setting for his "rags to riches" story — a distinct contrast to his earlier living conditions. He lived there alone and admitted to being lonely.

His book was a project he had talked about for years. And I felt confident writing his story for him. I was familiar with his background, family history and the chronology of his business endeavors, and — I thought I knew his story. But he surprised me. Behind the polished veneer of this extremely successful businessman, what I discovered was the real Gilbert Ortega. The inspirational Gilbert Ortega.

Sometimes even people you've known for years surprise you with a dimension of themselves you have yet to discover. That's the way it was with Gilbert. I gained a tremendous amount of respect for him. As his memoir developed, the business timelines and lively anecdotes evolved and began to showcase his strong message about perseverance. He believed in entrepreneurism — against all odds.

His story is an inspiration to anyone who has ever aspired to follow their dream.

Patricia Bezunartea

To the memory of
Gilbert Ortega
and his belief
in the American
spirit of entrepreneurship
and his appreciation of small business.

To the children of Gilbert Ortega, his successors:
Gayle Dean Ortega
Desirée L. Ortega
Gilbert D. Ortega, Jr.
F. Renée Ortega
and their mother, Linda VanderWagen Ortega.

The Journey

*"I have experienced the desperation of being busted
and broke, and felt the humiliation it served my ego.
But somehow I knew I couldn't give up,
so I kept trying, worked harder."*

When I leave home each morning headed for my Native American art galleries in downtown Scottsdale, I glance toward the end of the long palm-tree-lined driveway and focus on the old Navajo wagon that sits under a large mesquite tree there. Faded green paint curls and peels from its weathered wood, and the solid wheels seem to have sunk into the grass. To someone else it might seem out of place on the manicured grounds — not compatible with the affluent Paradise Valley surroundings.

But for me, that old Navajo wagon honors my humble reservation trading post beginnings, and symbolizes my personal struggle and the hard work and persistence it took to achieve success.

Looking at the wagon, I often reminisce — knowing I'm proud of the past and satisfied with the present. As I drive toward Old Scottsdale, I pass by impressive hotels and resorts that help make Scottsdale a prime tourist destination. I have shared in the development of the "West's Most Western Town" as it has become a sophisticated city filled with great shopping, fine restaurants, great golf courses — and a highly desirable place to live.

Most mornings, I arrive in Old Town early, long before any of the shops have opened, and usually drive along Brown Avenue and up Main Street, always observing, evaluating my stores and the other small businesses that are such an important part of our community. I park behind the Museum store where I have my office and wander into the store. There, in the silence and the soft light of the gallery not yet opened for business, I admire — with pride — beautiful pottery, rugs, baskets, jewelry.

Today, my business is one of the largest Native American arts and crafts enterprises in the country. The galleries showcase the finest artisans. Like me, these artisans are passionate about their work, and that is what keeps them getting better, producing finer creations. Each began by creating a simple piece of jewelry or a crude piece of pottery, for example, and as they continued to produce, their creativity soared and their quality improved. The same thing happened for me with my stores. I couldn't have developed my galleries without the years of experience and growth it took to get there.

Though I am proud of my accomplishments, it wasn't easy — and it didn't happen overnight, or without my share of failures. That is what success is all about — failure. In looking back, I realize that failure had a defining effect on every decision I made. I wouldn't trade any of those losses — those struggles — for anything. Later, *fear* of failure sometimes became my only competition. Staying on top is just as hard as getting there.

I have experienced the desperation of being busted and broke and felt the humiliation it served my ego. But somehow I knew I couldn't give up, so I kept trying, working harder. Since I didn't have financial backing, I had to become resourceful, clever, creative. Eventually, it began to pay off. My personal slogan became, "Early to bed, early to rise, work like hell and advertise."

And hard work produces amazing results. If an individual has the desire and perseverance to achieve success, he or she will. It doesn't require superior intelligence or family wealth, but it does require ambition, persistence, good judgment, and old-fashioned work, work, work.

Dreams can come true — but not by wishing on a star. And there are no short cuts.

When you talk to a self-made individual — if he or she has really worked for it — most often you'll see a humble person, someone who never forgets the hurdles, the lessons learned.

In 1966, Gilbert built Indian Village from 3rd-grade lumber and cinder block at an exit along a stretch of the new Interstate 40 in Lupton, Arizona.

By comparison, years later Gilbert studies and contemplates the merchandising of his new 10,000 square foot Museum Gallery on the corner of Scottsdale Road and Main Street in Old Town, 1998.

*A view of Gilbert's
3-acre Paradise Valley
estate.*

*An old Navajo wagon sits under
a tree near Gilbert's home – a
symbol of his humble beginnings.*

A Rolls Royce symbolizes Gilbert's business success,
while the Navajo wagon reflects his simple beginnings.

Frontier Life

"For a wiry, restless kid, I was quite shy. And I stuttered."

I was fortunate to be born into a strong, supportive, competitive family, a family overflowing with the spirit of entrepreneurship. As pioneers in Arizona Territory, my ancestors established themselves as sheep ranchers and Indian traders. By the time I came into the world four generations later, I guess the desire to be in business was in my blood.

Born in a small frame house in Holbrook, Arizona, I muscled my way into the world on April 19, 1936 — all 12 pounds of me. Twelve pounds of pure guts and determination.

I was the fifth child of Max and Amelia Ortega, the youngest for nearly 10 years before two more brothers were born. And I got a lot of attention. They even called me "Babito," because I was the baby the longest.

During those years I developed a special bond with my mother. She was a small energetic woman with bouncy brown hair, wise chocolate-brown eyes and a mischievous grin — and she was full of insight and understanding.

Dad was more serious, with strong handsome features and a friendly, approachable manner. And he was fueled by a desire to start his own business. But he didn't have much, and I was too young to know the work it took to make dreams come true. Dad told me it had been tough in the late 1930s. He thought the Depression would never end and felt that the steady stream of Okies he saw driving west with mattresses tied to their old cars proved it.

My father got a job at the Inspection Station on Route 66 at the Arizona-New Mexico state line where vehicles crossing into Arizona were checked. Since his job was nearly 70 miles from Holbrook, we moved to Lupton, Arizona and lived in a small house close to the Inspection Station. Just east of our place, the railroad tracks hummed with freight cars and passenger trains. Running parallel was Route 66, where dark sedans, like giant beetles, crawled along the highway and trucks filled with goods from the east traveled west. To enter Arizona, they had to pass through the Inspection Station.

Dad wore a uniform and a metal badge. To a little kid like me, he looked official, and I thought he was very important, like a sheriff or a marshal.

Lupton was like a swirl of dust in the heart of the huge expanse that was the Navajo reservation, where rugged red cliffs towered above a landscape of scruffy brush, juniper and piñon trees. Navajo hogans blended with the earth, a few boxy little houses dotted the area, and a small store sold a few groceries. Nearby, Navajos in horse-drawn wagons lumbered along dusty roads. Sheep and goats munched lazily on tufts of wild grasses while sheep dogs napped in the sun.

The Navajos were our neighbors, and they also became our friends.

I spent a lot of time out there, running and playing in that vast openness. But, for a wiry, restless kid, I was quite shy. And I stuttered. I don't know if I was shy because I stuttered or I stuttered because I was shy. It would clutch at me. Breathing in gasps, I was unable to get the words out. Sometimes I blamed my stuttering on my brother Armand. He was eight years older than me and would hold me down and pound on my chest with his fist. But he said he did that to *stop* my stuttering. Mom never called attention to my stuttering. That would have increased my frustration. It wasn't until years later when Mom and Dad bought me a guitar for my twelfth birthday, and I began to play and sing, that the stuttering lifted and I gained a new avenue of expression.

Maybe stuttering quieted me in a way that made me more observant. It probably contributed to my shyness, too. I've struggled with shyness since childhood. In spite of that, I've felt a desire to succeed and had a sense of competition for as long as I can remember.

And Mom's lighthearted ways helped me develop a good sense of humor, too. She loved to tease and play jokes on us. So did Armand.

For example, one afternoon I ran into the house where my brothers Armand, Maxie, and Aggie were gathered around the table. I couldn't have been more than five years old.

"Gilbert, look. Mom made us ice cream," Armand said motioning to the bowls in front of them piled high with creamy whiteness. I glanced toward my place at the table where only a couple of small spoonfuls sat in my bowl. Like any five-year-old, I loved ice cream, and it was a rare treat.

I stomped over to my sorry serving. I could almost taste the cool, smooth vanilla ice cream melting in my mouth. But, seeing those few little spoonfuls, I was mad at being cheated out of my fair share.

Armand knew I was angry and he held his arm out to stop me as I approached the bowl.

"Gilbert, Gilbert, don't be mad. We were just tricking you. It's mashed potatoes."

Then I *really* got mad. I had counted on ice cream. Everybody laughed. It hurt me to be fooled. I didn't want to be tricked or have to laugh at myself to cover up my true feelings.

The whole thing had been Mom's idea. She had made such fluffy, creamy mashed potatoes that to her they looked like ice cream. Armand went along with it and they fooled me — and it worked.

Growing up, I came to understand that things weren't always what they appeared. I learned to be curious, to observe, to question. Then, as I got older, I instigated those kinds of jokes myself.

We didn't have much in Lupton, but Mom was always with us in that little house, making sure we were well fed and cared for — four energetic boys and one girl. That was my sister Esther, the oldest of the family. I thought she was the prettiest girl around. So did Sonny McCarrell. They got married when she was 15. She seemed all grown up and sophisticated to me.

And we four boys, Armand, Maxie, Aggie and me, thrived in our wilderness world.

Mom and Dad loved and respected each other, and they had an excellent relationship. I could feel it. And they wanted the best for us, too. Mom knew exactly how to handle Dad, and she never allowed us to be disrespectful of him. If one of us boys did, she would catch whoever it was — even if the culprit had fallen asleep, he would get a well-deserved swat with the broom. And Mom would never go against Dad. She would say, "What do you think, Max? Should the kids do this or that?" She used psychology. She knew how to approach him the right way.

Gilbert's father, Max, Sr. in uniform at Arizona's Inspection Station, 1942.

Brothers: Gilbert, Aggie and Max, Jr. wearing hats of other inspectors.

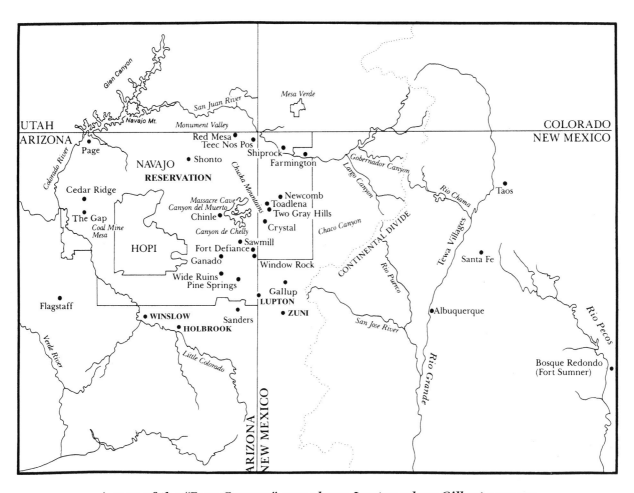

A map of the "Four Corners" area shows Lupton where Gilbert grew up.

Shoe Shines for Nickels and Dimes

*"I guess that's about as entrepreneurial as a kid could get
in Holbrook in the 1940s."*

For whatever reason, after a few years, we moved back to Holbrook. I remember Dad saying it was a change in administrations — from Democrat to Republican. He said as far as he knew, there was only one Republican in Apache County, so why all the uproar?

I hadn't remembered much about Holbrook — since I was little more than a toddler when we left. But it seemed that by the time we moved back, I was related to half the residents. We squeezed into a two-bedroom, green frame house "across the river." That's what they called the poor section of town, south of the Little Colorado.

Holbrook was an old railroad, ranching and reservation town with an outlaw past. It was founded in 1881 when the railroad arrived. The town had originally been called "Horsehead Crossing," but the railroad decided to name it after the chief railroad engineer, Henry R. Holbrook.

The windblown town's buildings were as strong as its people, made of brick, stone and petrified wood. And the place really was filled with Ortega relatives. Uncle Tony, Dad's brother, was a sheriff's deputy, and sometimes he would give my brothers and me a ride home in the squad car. Uncle Santos, another of Dad's brothers, owned a busy store in town. Relatives spilled out of Concho, into Holbrook, on toward Phoenix, and beyond — relatives with names like Baca, Peralta, Candelaria, Castillo, and more. There were hundreds. They were always visiting, having coffee, sharing meals, storytelling, laughing. And music filled the air, with Mom playing the banjo and Dad the accordion. I tended to stay in the background. Our family was so large that I had aunts and cousins who were the same age as me — and I had become an uncle by the time I was about 7. It all seemed perfectly normal to me.

Dad taught us our family history early on — a proud heritage. We were pioneers. I was a fourth generation Arizonan. My great-grandfather, Santos

Ortega, and his wife had settled in Concho in the 1880s when it was Arizona Territory. There, in that fertile shell-like valley, he — like many of the other original Spanish settlers — built a solid business as a sheep rancher and wool trader. Their family was large, and the children married within the Concho community. Many of the settlers had come from New Mexico. Recently, family genealogists have traced our Ortega roots in New Mexico as far back as the 1600s.

My grandfather, Tomás Ortega, continued the Concho sheep tradition, but eventually moved to Holbrook. Overgrazing was taking its toll on the area and the business had reached a saturation point. There was a time when over 100,000 sheep grazed near Concho in the area that later became the Petrified Forest National Park. Dad said my Grandpa Tomás, his father, eventually opened a trading post at Bitahochee near Chambers on the Navajo reservation, and Dad helped him in the store.

That's what Dad wanted, too — his own store. It was his dream, and he was determined to achieve it, and that excited me.

I suppose the desire to be in business really was in my blood, because by the time I was 9, I decided I'd build a shoeshine box and try to make a few dollars shining shoes. I guess that was about as entrepreneurial as a kid could get in Holbrook in the 1940s, although my brother Armand had done well selling newspapers. I made the kit with some scrap wood and sanded and smoothed it. I enjoyed making my shoeshine box and was proud of myself. Our folks taught us to always do the best we could with what we had available. My only monetary investment was buying two tins of Shinola shoe polish – one black and one brown for about a dime each; a soft brush for probably 15 cents; and a polishing cloth for about a nickel; as well as a few rags that Mom gave me. For 40 cents or less I was in business. Armand lent me the money, and he's been asking me for half of everything I've made ever since!

Mom saw me off that first summer Saturday in the shoe shining business. I listened as she gave me some last bits of advice. "Be respectful, Gilbert. Greet people nicely and do the best job you can. And always say thank you."

I agreed.

"This is the happiest day of my life," I sighed.

A bright grin spread across her face and her eyes crinkled up in the corners the way they did when she laughed.

I grabbed my shoe shine kit filled with supplies and my makeshift cardboard sign — *SHOE SHINE, 10 CENTS* — and headed for the center of town.

I turned to see my mom still waving goodbye from the front door. Dogs and chickens wandered the dirt street like they had a destination, too. As I ran toward the bridge, I glanced back again, but our tiny house had disappeared behind the bushy tamaracks that lined the Little Colorado. A powdery trail of dust hung in the air behind me — Holbrook was a dusty town. That was an advantage for a kid in the shoe-shining business.

"This *is* the happiest day of my life," I whispered.

I crossed the old bridge that led to the railroad tracks, which I quickly skipped across, then on to Center Street, and gazed at Uncle Santos' store. The entire front was inlaid with huge chunks of petrified wood that glistened like swirls of chocolate and caramel in the June morning sun. Two gas pumps stood out front. I imagined how wonderful it would be to have my own store someday. Sometimes I would wander through there with hands stuffed in my empty pockets, studying the wares. But not today.

I needed a busy place to set up and, as I rounded the corner onto Route 66 — Holbrook's main street — I decided the best location was in front of the Roxy Theater. It was across from Camel's Steak House where Armand used to sell newspapers. Holbrook bustled with business on Saturdays, especially in the summer. It was in the center of ranch country and adjacent to the Navajo and Hopi reservations and lots of folks headed to town for supplies and staples, and maybe a shoe shine.

With my kit and sign in place, I leaned against the wall and stared at people's shoes as they ambled up and down the street. Kids from school waved as they went into the theater for the morning western.

Nervous, fidgeting, I began to pace. I wanted to march up to someone and ask, "Need a shoe shine, sir?" But I just couldn't. I was too shy.

Determined, I anchored myself at my post. I remembered my grandfather Tomás Ortega saying, "If you want to sell something and you stand on a corner with it long enough, you'll sell it."

So I stood there.

Finally, a prospect stepped up with some dusty, scuffed-up boots. I cleaned them off, slathered them with polish and shined them up like new. It helped business to have people actually see me shining shoes. I thanked him and slipped the two nickels into my pocket. It felt good to have a sale.

Tourists drove by with license plates from states I had only read about. Some stopped for gas or food, but they were not likely interested in shoe shines. Mostly, they would slow down and stare at Navajos loading supplies into their horse-drawn wagons.

Little by little, I gained momentum. I shined everything from cowboy boots and work boots to church shoes. By 5 p.m., I had about $1.40. Since the next movie at the Roxy would start at 7 p.m., I decided to stay open for business until then. Maybe some of the moviegoers would need shines. Every so often, I stuck my hand in my pocket and jingled the change. It felt so good to hold onto all those dimes and nickels.

By 7 p.m., I had $1.80. I picked up my portable store and headed home. I knew better than to stay out later. As dusk approached, there was always the threat of *La Llorona* appearing along the river. My mother and aunts had told me the legend of the wailing woman, a widow who had drowned her children in the river so she would be free to marry a man who later rejected her.

"Her ghost returns as darkness falls, always crying and sobbing, looking for a child to snap up and take with her," my mother would repeat.

Even though I knew it was a fable, a chill ran up my spine as I ran across the bridge. A burst of wind swept past me, and I peered into the shadowy tamaracks along the river — just in case — and then darted down the dusty pathway.

From the road, our tiny green frame house seemed welcoming, friendly, safe. The house looked square and short, with a brick chimney peeking above the nearly flat roof. I made a quick trip to the outhouse before running inside to relate the day's success.

My mother turned from the wood stove and smiled as the door opened. Dad leaned forward in his chair, away from the radio where he was listening intently to a boxing match.

I dug my hand in my pocket and piled the change on the table next to the radio.

"A dollar and eighty cents," I told him.

"That's good for your first time, son. When people get to know you're there all the time, they'll plan on a shoe shine and business will only get better," Dad advised.

So, I shined shoes until we moved back to Lupton a year later when Dad went back to work at the Inspection Station.

Gilbert's great grandparents Santos Ortega and Anna Maria Apodoca Ortega, settled in Concho, Arizona Territory in the 1880s.

Gilbert's grandparents, Tomás Ortega and Pablita Peralta Ortega with daughter Auralia, approx. 1894, Concho, Arizona Territory.

Gilbert's grandparents and growing family in front of their house, Concho, Arizona Territory, 1905 From left: Auralia, Arsenia, Pablita, Tomas, Regina, Santos, Tom.

Tomás used wooden trade coins as a form of barter in his trading post.

Tomás Ortega, Gilbert's grandfather opened a trading post at Bitahochee north of Chambers, Arizona, approx. 1915.

Gilbert's uncle, Santos Ortega's store in Holbrook, Arizona, 1940s.

Under the Giant Lupton Sky

"The Navajos made the best wagons, and I wondered what it would be like someday for me to own a wagon and a couple of horses. I would be on top of the world then, I thought."

Back in Lupton, Dad discovered that the Atchison, Topeka and Santa Fe Railroad owned 160 acres of land, right there in what was called the checkerboard area of the reservation — parcels of private land tucked into the vast Navajo nation.

He needed to find a way to buy it, but didn't know whom to approach. Nevertheless, he continued to inquire.

Soon, winter brought icy wind and blowing snow to the region. Route 66 became slippery and dangerous, especially one night when Dad was on duty at the Inspection Station. Someone passing through told him a car had slid off the highway. A while later another traveler reported the same incident and said that it looked like the man needed help. He could freeze to death out there. Dad knew the location and drove down to where the car was stuck. He offered to help, but realized he could do nothing about the car until daylight. The man was freezing, so Dad brought him back to his post. Soon the warmth of the toasty inspection station, a few cups of steaming coffee and the last of the doughnuts revived him. The man expressed his thanks. He said if Dad hadn't helped him, he might have frozen to death out there in that icy blackness.

With a few hours until daylight, they got to talking. Dad told him about his business plans and his growing family. As it turned out, the man was a railroad executive on a business trip. Dad was amazed by the coincidence and told him about the property he wanted to buy — that it was owned by the railroad. As dawn approached, he pointed to the spot where the 160 acres of rugged land stretched from the railroad tracks to the west across Route 66, over the muddy swath of the Rio Puerco, past the sandstone outcropping of Battleship Mountain, to the edge of the Navajo reservation. Like this property, Dad explained that patches of deeded land in this checkerboard area were hard to find.

While Dad drove him back to rescue his car, the gentleman assured Dad that he would find out who at the ATSF Railroad handled land sales and if it could be purchased. He would do everything he could to make it happen. He said he owed him the favor. The men shook hands and Dad said he felt positive and hopeful that he could buy the land.

And he did. I'm not really sure how much he paid, but at most it was a few thousand dollars. Then he sold almost 40 acres to Uncle Santos. That gave him enough money to start building the store he always wanted.

The perfect spot for the store faced Route 66, and the building would sit on the north side of the highway. Most travelers were coming west, and it would be a highly visible and logical location. There was a buzz of excitement about planning the store. I was amazed at Dad's ingenuity. What he lacked in cash he made up for in creativity. He heard there was a stockpile of ammunition boxes for sale at Ft. Wingate, which lies just east of Gallup, New Mexico. Ft. Wingate had served as an ammunition depot during WWII, so there were lots of these thick, heavy, natural pine crates approximately three feet long by a foot square — and they were selling for about 25 cents each. Dad's price range! He bought several loads and hauled them back to Lupton.

The ammunition boxes were stenciled with different letters or numbers, and I asked him what they meant.

"Those are ordnance numbers, son. You see," he said pointing to the lettering, "These held 30-caliber and those M-1's."

I watched the sturdy crates become the framework of the store. Friends from the Inspection Station and relatives from Holbrook helped nail the boxes together, one on top of the other, then connected sections, side by side. The building took on a nice rectangular shape that resembled the dimensions of the ammunition boxes. The store stretched about 60 feet across the front and 20 feet deep. With cheap lumber and white plaster, they finished the inside and outside walls, assembled a wooden floor, and supported the flat roof with two-by-fours, topped with plywood and roofing paper.

Dad installed a propane tank, then dug a small well by hand. We couldn't get any water, though, so we had to haul it from the well next to the railroad section house. Inside the store, a crank-up phone connected us to the operator. Outside, an outhouse connected us to reality. Dad put up a basketball hoop close by and from then on basketball consumed every free moment we had.

A small living area at the back of the store had one bedroom for Mom and Dad and the new baby, my brother Denny. Armand, Maxie, Aggie, and I stayed in a little shack behind the store. It was comfortable that first summer, but even the wood stove in there barely broke the chill when the freezing winter months hit. Later Dad bought a railroad house close by for more room.

Dad had a local Navajo artist letter "Indian Trails Trading Post" across the front of the building and paint colorful thunderbirds, kachinas, and rainbow *Yei* dancers, all around, as well as bright signs for curios and gasoline.

At the far end of the building stood two gravity-fed gas pumps — one for regular, one for ethyl — gas sold at about 24 cents a gallon, unless there was a gas war and the prices dropped. Later, Dad built a gas house of cinder block near the pumps for supplies, oil, and tires.

Inside the store, they hammered up shelves and built a counter where Dad put an adding machine with a cash box attached.

We helped pound homemade signs into the hard earth along the highway — signs letting travelers know we had gasoline, curios, food. We boys would pump gas and help mark merchandise and stock shelves.

The Navajos were a key element of the business, too. They needed a convenient place to trade for food and supplies, plus the store saved them the 20-mile wagon trip to Gallup.

When Dad opened the store in June, 1946, the shelf displays were meager. To buy groceries, he went to Gallup and talked to Basilio DeGregorio, who owned California Supermarket. Basilio gave him a discount. At first he could only buy four or five sacks of flour, a few tins of lard, beans, salt, bacon, salt pork, and some coffee and sugar. He bought about a dozen cans of stewed tomatoes – because the Navajos loved them – some canned peaches, canned milk, soda pop and candy bars. And he would pick up a few things for Mom, because she didn't drive.

Little by little, Dad broadened his selection and purchased larger quantities and established accounts with regional dry goods companies. Eventually, he bought bolts of velvet in deep red, cobalt and burgundy and denim jeans. He carried lanterns and oil, tinware bowls and mugs, and other supplies for the Navajo lifestyle. Later, he put in a cooler to hold big rolls of bologna and huge wheels of longhorn cheese.

Soon, salesmen and novelty dealers stopped at the trading post, and Dad ordered inexpensive curio items from them — things like salt and pepper shakers, costume jewelry, gifts and souvenirs. He ordered beaded belts and toy tomahawks and feather headdresses. And he always had a supply of canvas water bags that travelers strapped to the front of their cars in case the radiator overheated on those summer treks across the high desert. He attracted tourists traveling along the highway — Route 66 was the only paved road around. And the store served our Navajo neighbors, too. The Navajos were good neighbors.

Under the giant sky, their horse-drawn wagons carved dirt pathways that wound their way where necessary — and most reservation roads in the area led to Lupton. Hogans dotted the landscape, blending with the elements. The traditional eight-sided log dwelling with its domed earthen roof fit naturally in the environment. The Navajo way was beautiful and simple, like the hogan door which traditionally opened to the east to greet the morning sun. Inside the hogan, solid dirt floors packed stone-hard gave way to a heavy blackened wood stove which sat in the middle and mats for sleeping spread around the outer edges of the floor against the walls. Four or five people could easily live there.

The Steven's family hogan sat east of the store, beyond the railroad tracks. Freddie Stevens was studying to be a medicine man. The Upshaw and the Morgan hogans were close by, too. Joe and Benny Upshaw became my great friends. So did Louie Morgan. Actually, we were friends with all the local Navajos. The Smiths lived a little further out on the reservation, and one day after they had been in the store, I rode home with Charlie in their wagon. I stared out into the vast openness, out to where the weathered red rock cliffs sat in the distance. Up close, the junipers and piñons, twisted by years of constant wind, stood as hearty as the Navajo people who were the soul of the environment. The movement of the horses rocked the wagon along the path.

The Navajos made the best wagons, and I wondered what it would be like someday for me to own a wagon and a couple of horses. I would be on top of the world then, I thought.

Another time when I rode out to the Smith's hogan, I ate horse meat with them. It tasted just fine to me. I had eaten fry bread and mutton stew a lot of times. But that was probably the only time I ever ate horse meat.

Some of the Navajos traveled so far by wagon to buy supplies at Indian Trails Trading Post that they had to spend the night.

The trading post became a natural gathering place for the Navajos — and a natural highway stop for tourists. Dad traded for jewelry and rugs from the local Navajos, and he allowed them to buy on credit. Some received small government stipend checks that they would use as payment, too. And Dad learned to speak "trader Navajo." We all learned to speak some Navajo and we picked up some of their mannerisms. For example, pointing a finger was considered bad manners, so Navajos pointed with their lips — stuck their lips out and made kind of a puffing noise — I still do it.

We learned a lot from the Navajos and a lot about the Navajos themselves.

We were taught to respect everyone and treat people well — to always say "Sir" or "Ma'am," and to shake hands with anyone we met.

"Don't ever talk about anybody; the banana peel might be under your own foot," Dad always advised. "God bless everybody."

Dad taught us to appreciate the jewelry and crafts of our Navajo neighbors — crafts he bought and traded for. I noticed how closely Dad inspected jewelry, checking the bezels that held the turquoise stones, looking carefully at the stamping and the soldering. He said a good silversmith could easily set up shop with a hammer, a chisel, a tree stump, and a blow torch. Design and skill were important. There was natural talent everywhere, he would tell us. Many Navajo families made the same style of jewelry and worked together.

Our entire family worked together, too. I started pumping gas when I was 10. Maxie and Aggie pumped gas, too. Dad paid us, but I got less because I was the most inexperienced. I also helped in the store, mostly stocking shelves.

Armand worked for Leroy and Jake Atkinson a couple of miles east at Box Canyon, just across the Arizona/New Mexico state line. He pumped gas, stocked shelves. Leroy had Navajo silversmiths making jewelry there, and Armand learned a lot from him. The Atkinsons would become life-long friends.

By then Armand had a car — a Pontiac with a little trailer on the back to haul barrels of water. I would go with him to fill the barrels at the well next to the railroad section house across the tracks. One time we had filled two barrels, and as we bumped over the tracks toward the store, one of the barrels rolled off and stuck in the middle of the tracks — and a train was heading right for us, about a half mile away and began whistling feverishly. We jumped out of the car, hopped over the tracks and heaved that barrel onto the trailer as fast as we could and towed it off the tracks — just in time. After that incident, Mom quickly made sure we got our own working well.

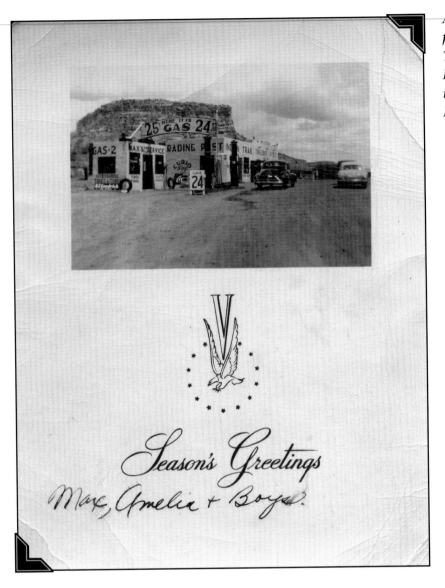

A view of Gilbert's father's Indian Trails Trading Post with Battleship Mountain in the background, Lupton, 1947.

A typical scene of life on the Navajo reservation in the late 1940s.

Trading Post Kid

"Dad paid me $3.00 a week to work. In retrospect, I think he was giving me $3.00 a week to learn how to work."

In the summer, Dad opened the store at daybreak, and it was quiet and dim as the first rays of dawn touched our world. On my way out to the gas pumps, I would usually grab a strawberry soda pop and a bag of peanuts, and pour the peanuts into the bottle and shake it up a little. That was my fuel. It would keep me going for hours. Sometimes I would lean against the front of the trading post, absorbed in the peach-colored dawn sky — daydreaming, munching on peanuts and sipping strawberry pop. Dad paid me $3.00 a week to work. In retrospect, I think he was giving me $3.00 a week to learn *how* to work.

I headed over to check the amount of gasoline in the glass receptacles at the top of the gravity-fed pumps. To be prepared for business, I pumped each one up to ten gallons. Then I tucked my shirt into my jeans and smoothed down my hair and stared down the highway looking for cars.

The long stretch of road cut an asphalt pathway through our borderline corner of Arizona. When travelers stopped, they were always curious about the vast landscape, the Navajo Indians and their hogans — the homes they lived in — and they continually asked about the snakes crossing the road. Sometimes they would run over them. "Those are rattlesnakes," I would tell them. "Rattlers."

As I stared onto the pavement looking for rattlesnakes, a clever moneymaking idea popped into my head. I ran into the house and grabbed the rattle out of my baby brother Denny's crib, then snapped up an empty moccasin box from the back of the store. Quickly, I lettered a small sign: *SEE REAL BABY RATTLER — 10 CENTS*. I cut a flap in the top of the box, bent it back, then folded it back down again to create a peephole. I doubled the sign over and set it on the corner of the box. Then I placed the box in an obvious spot by the gas pumps, where I waited for customers.

Soon, travelers showed up to buy gas and wander into the store. And I began pocketing dimes. Most of the tourists got a kick out of it, especially kids watching their dad peer into the box — poised to jump back — then see an ordinary baby rattle.

It took a few hours for my dad to find out that people were paying me 10 cents to peek into a box and see my brother's baby rattle instead of a snake. He marched out of the store and headed over to me and put an end to my fake snake scheme. He was embarrassed that I was trying to trick people. I thought I was being clever, and I did make some extra money. But I realized he was right. I promised him I wouldn't trick a customer again. I never did.

By the time I put the rattle back in Denny's crib, my mother knew the story and she gave me a disapproving look, but when she turned away I could see her eyes crinkle up the way they did when she laughed.

Soon I began getting more jobs in the trading post. While I stocked shelves in the store, I paid attention to how my dad handled people. He made customers feel comfortable, and he was a fine judge of character. He had good instincts about people. I also enjoyed watching tourists shop; I was interested in what they would purchase. I realized people liked to buy what they *wanted,* much more than they liked to buy what they *needed.* Besides, being a tourist was fun, like having a license to buy salt and pepper shakers, kids' headdresses, rubber tomahawks, postcards. The bigger and better sales, though, were Indian jewelry or Navajo rugs. Buyers were serious about those lasting purchases. And the locale couldn't help but inspire them to buy quality momentos of their trip.

Sometimes I would wander through the trading post trying to imagine how good it would feel to take in a couple of hundred dollars a day like Dad did. I learned quickly that that wasn't profit. And Dad had to put every cent back into inventory, to build stock and, hopefully, to fill the store with more merchandise.

After our first summer on Route 66, Dad hired Armand to work full time in the store since he had graduated from high school and had experience working for the Atkinsons. Besides, Dad had offered to drive the school bus mornings and afternoons. The elementary and high schools were in Sanders, about 30 miles west. Since Lupton was the beginning and end of the bus route, someone from the school board asked Dad to do the job. It seemed to make sense to me since he was always civic-minded.

So Dad drove the school bus for about five years. Maxie, Aggie, and I would hop on board about 7 a.m. Then he picked up everyone around the trading post area, like the Upshaws and Louie Morgan. Dad stopped at designated places along the highway, seemingly desolate spots where you'd never expect to see a group of reservation kids waiting for a school bus.

When school started, I could feel the change of season in the air. A cool breeze announced the approach of fall, and possibly a long, cold winter.

It took about an hour to get to school. Sanders was located at the intersection of Route 66 and the road to St. Johns and Concho. Sanders elementary and the high school sat on the mesa top. Frame houses dotted the nearby area, and hogans were nestled into the open landscape of the reservation.

We would jump off the bus and race to our classrooms. Our books were on loan from the school and we tied them together with whatever we had — twine, leather, a belt. All the students dressed the best they could. And we got to eat hot lunches at the school cafeteria. About 25 kids were in each class, and the curriculum was basic to any school, even though the mix of students was unique. Though classes were taught in English, Navajo was the first language of many of my classmates.

Still shy and afraid of stuttering, I hated to be called on in class, even though I usually knew the answer. I was especially good in math.

On the bus rides home, the change of season became more noticeable. Fall captured the area. The rabbit brush and high desert vegetation burst into yellows and purples, and the sunlight softened its glow across the openness. Even the wind seemed to calm. And all eyes were on the piñon trees. Would they produce this year? When a good crop hit, a new economy took shape.

In late October as the school bus bumped along, Dad pointed to some wagons sitting out by a stand of piñons. That signaled a piñon crop. The Navajos would place blankets under a tree and then shake the tree to loosen the ripe cones so they would fall onto the blankets. I thought that was resourceful. Then the hard work began. Nestled inside each segment of the cone was a small dark pine nut. And each segment had to be opened by hand to encourage the piñon out of hiding. It was a labor-intensive and pine-sap-sticky chore. But it was a cash crop.

Dad bought piñons, and wool, too — by the pound. Sometimes the Navajos would hide rocks in the sacks so they would weigh more. Dad knew how to handle these situations beautifully. He taught us how to deal with people, without being taken advantage of.

I loved piñon season, because Mom would roast the tiny nuts in a cast iron skillet on the wood stove. She put a little water and salt in the pan and carefully toasted a layer of nuts. After they cooled a bit, I would grab a handful and break into each nut with a quick snap of my teeth. Roasting brought out the wonderful flavor of the cream-colored nuggets.

When we got home from school, those fall afternoons were devoted to shooting baskets while we watched for gas customers. Maxie, Aggie, Joe Upshaw, Louie Morgan, and me played hour after hour shooting baskets. If I was alone or pumping gas, I would practice — shooting baskets over and over again. I became a pretty good basketball player. Our court was dirt, of course, the surface hardened by our pounding feet. It was our "Play Station."

It was probably around then that Louie Morgan came to live with us. Both of his parents suffered the scourge of the Navajos — alcoholism. Because they were always drunk, Louie spent most of his time with us, and Dad said he could even come live with us if he wanted. He was about 13 then. Louie was tall and handsome, bright, funny, and an excellent athlete. With us, he was safe and well cared for. We took to introducing him as our brother. That's what it felt like. Louie thrived, and I learned how important it is to recognize people's needs, and how important it is to help the community that becomes your family.

Even though Louie was raised with us, as an adult, he never wandered from the Navajo Way or left his roots on the reservation. And he continued to pursue athletics, even participating in senior softball on a national level.

Many other close friendships developed around the area, too, and as business on the highway slowed in the fall, people had a little more time to visit. Leroy Atkinson, or his brother Jake, would stop by for coffee with Dad and catch up on commerce. Everyone was trying to get ahead, and they had a lot in common. Leroy was a good businessman and a good person. He always chewed on a cigar — never smoked it — it just hung there in his mouth. Jake, who had suffered polio, had such a magical personality that it overcame the appearance of the crippling results he had endured from polio. Joe, Leroy's son, would come along too. While Leroy visited with Dad and Armand, Joe would play basketball outside with us, or sometimes we would climb the hills and mesas.

Joe was a few years younger than me and the youngest of the four kids in his family. But we became friends and established a life-long business relationship, too. He had a great personality and a quick wit. Years later we would tease each other about our long connection. In social situations around other traders in Gallup, I would exaggerate Joe's childhood arrivals in Lupton, saying he drove up with his dad and had his leg propped out the car window, showing off his new cowboy boots, and resting his arm on the door to flash his fancy fringed Roy Rogers gloves. He even wore a badge. When I told the story, I pretended I had been jealous of Joe because he was a rich kid and that my Roy Rogers gloves and boots had been tattered hand-me-downs. Joe always went along with it and we had fun. No one was sure whether to believe us or not.

Even though Joe lived just a couple of miles away at Box Canyon, where they had their store, it was across the state line in New Mexico, so he didn't go to school with us. Leroy and his wife had moved there from Texas during WWII. Dad said that the war effort had halted most manufacturing — even cars weren't available — and no jewelry was being produced, except Indian jewelry. Native Americans were allowed to continue making jewelry because it was their living. So, Leroy had taken advantage of that opportunity and set up a group of Navajo silversmiths. He bought silver, which only came in 1-ounce squares then and had to be pounded out on an anvil. And he bought blow torches to heat the silver. Leroy set up production and started a wholesale operation. Then he encouraged his brothers, Jake and Herman, to move west and learn the business. Later, Armand would learn a lot, as well, while working with the Atkinsons.

Since our trading post was so accessible, people would stop by often — relatives, friends, neighbors. They would gather at the kitchen table and drink coffee, and Mom always had something simmering on the stove to serve guests, or would offer pop or snacks from the store. We were always welcome to help ourselves to a soda pop or a candy bar — but knew not to take advantage.

Once in a while, Art Beasley would come and visit Dad, too. He was married to a Navajo woman from the area, and they had a big family. Dad always spoke highly of him. Mr. Beasley sold petrified wood further west of us down the highway at Querino Canyon. He skillfully hand-cut paperweights, bookends and ashtrays. When he stopped by, he would have all the kids with him and they would pile out of his truck and we would play basketball together while our dads visited. For me, playing basketball was a great way for a shy kid to make friends. When Mr. Beasley was ready to leave, he simply tooted a whistle he had installed on his truck, and the kids would run and jump in the back and head home. Like a flash, they were gone. We never knew when to expect them, but we always had fun when they showed up.

When the Beasley kids grew up, they took their mother's name, Yellowhorse, and developed different facets of the Indian arts and crafts business — even in Lupton.

Gilbert began pumping gas at his dad's trading post when he was 10.

Gilbert also stocked shelves and learned to work in the store.

Armand, 13, pumping gas in Lupton.

As a teenager, Armand worked with Jake Atkinson at Box Canyon Trading Post near Lupton.

Horsing Around

"I was pumping gas the next morning when Leroy dropped Joe off, lugging a heavy canvas sack of change."

By the time I was 11, I had a job near the Inspection Station, feeding and caring for a horse that belonged to one of the inspection workers. I wanted a bicycle so I could ride there, and I had saved almost enough money to buy one. So Dad took me to B.F. Goodrich in Gallup, and even pitched in a little money to help me buy a used bike. I was proud of that bicycle, and as I peddled along the usually dry river bed, I bounced it up and down like a stallion. The Puerco offered the best pathway to avoid the scruffy brush and short clumps of cactus of the high desert, and the bike made for a quick half-mile ride to the Inspection Station. Horses were still an important part of reservation life. The mare was due to foal soon, and she was in a corral close by the state line with some other horses. I would feed her, brush her, exercise her. The owner had promised me the foal as payment. When the colt was born, I named him "Sandy" for his earthy color, and I brought him home after he was weaned.

I took good care of Sandy, and soon it was time to break him. My brothers and I gathered behind the store in the wash — that's what we called the Puerco — trying to break Sandy, but, of course, we didn't have a saddle, a bridle, or a bit — just a rope. It seemed like a safe place to break the horse and a softer fall if any of us got thrown. We just took turns jumping onto his back and holding onto his mane or the rope. As light as I was, I got thrown off right away into the dust. Maxie tried. He was bigger and stronger, but couldn't stay on. Neither could Louie. It took Aggie to do it. Aggie towered over the rest of us. He was big, strong, and muscular, and just too much for Sandy to buck off.

Between Sandy and my bike, *local* transportation was a snap for me.

Joe Atkinson seemed to have taken an interest in Sandy, admiring him every time he stopped by. About a year passed, and many visits later, Joe approached me with a business proposition — the first of many for us.

"How much do you want for Sandy?" Joe asked.

He wanted to buy Sandy, though I hadn't really thought about selling him.

"Fifty dollars," I replied. Though I guess I would have taken $25.

Joe said he had already discussed it with his dad, and Leroy told Joe he could have all the change in their pop machine to buy the horse. Joe said it hadn't been emptied in a while.

Now that pop machine saw a lot of business, because the bus stopped at Box Canyon, and people coming and going bought soda pop. I wondered how much money might be in there. It was worth a chance, so I took the deal.

I was pumping gas the next morning when Leroy dropped Joe off, lugging a heavy canvas sack of change. We sunk down in the dirt next to the pumps and started counting. First we separated nickels and dimes into heaps, then stacked them into one-dollar piles. It took almost all day — and a few sodas and candy bars — and it totaled about $50. This was a lot of money for me and I hoped Dad would convert it into bills. Dad hoped I would do something wise with it, like buy a few pieces of jewelry or maybe a Navajo rug. And I did just that.

I jogged to get Sandy at the side of the store where I had him tied to a tree. Joe hopped on and rode him home. He planned to hitch him up behind their store until his dad could build him a little corral.

A few mornings later, however, Sandy was gone.

Joe looked everywhere for him — all around Box Canyon. His call for Sandy echoed through Box Canyon, over and over, while he combed the confined area. Since Joe couldn't find Sandy in the most likely place, he figured the horse must have gotten loose and gone back to Lupton. But he hadn't, and Joe couldn't believe Sandy was gone.

I helped him look for Sandy all around Lupton, but he was nowhere. We never found the horse. Some Navajo neighbors told Joe they thought Sandy had gotten hit by a train. Together, we looked for Sandy for years. I think Joe is still looking for him.

It was several years later when I bought another horse. He was old and sway-backed. I was convinced I could sell him to my brother Dewey's friend, Freddie Slatten. I called him "Lightning," so Freddie would automatically think he was a fast horse. When I showed him to Freddie, I got underneath him a little and pushed up his back so he would look better.

I knew Freddie was able to get money, because by then his dad, Jim Slatten, had a small nightclub in Lupton. And Freddie bought Lightning. This horse didn't disappear. He couldn't!

A Change of Tune

"I never stuttered when I sang. My vocal chords relaxed and I could just sing. Singing helped my confidence, too. My bouts of stuttering lessened dramatically."

When I was 12, my youngest brother Dewey was born. Even though Mom was a busy homemaker, she still helped Dad in the store, too. She always made time for me and encouraged me. Every child needs someone to believe in them, so they can believe in themselves. Encouragement was Mom's gift to me. Dad gave me opportunity.

I marked merchandise, continued to stock shelves and pump gas, even waited on customers. By then I had started dreaming about my own store, the way city kids dream of lemonade stands, I guess — only I wanted a trading post. Well, that was all I knew.

I got to know the salesmen who called on Dad, people like Bernarr DePriest and Bob Petley. I became aware of what was going on around me. I was curious.

Riding my bike around Lupton offered an interesting perspective of the world. There in front of the Stevens' hogan I could see Bertha standing over a cast iron pot of herbs she had boiled to create a *vegetal* dye. She used different plants and herbs to achieve a variety of earthy colors. When the dye was just right, she removed the herbs, then dropped her hand-spun yarn into the vat. The cream-colored wool yarn soaked up the dye for a rug she was about to weave. Her vertical loom, made of tree branches, stood next to a juniper tree. A large basket stuffed with bundles of natural yarn and tools sat nearby. It held everything from sheep shears and wire-toothed wool carders, to a long spindle which she used to deftly spin the yarn, and hand-whittled hardwood combs whose tines matched the spacing of the warp threads on her loom.

I remember wishing I could buy a rug from Bertha someday.

Freddie Stevens sat a short distance away, pulverizing gypsum for a sandpainting. He would combine gypsum with sandstone, charcoal, cornmeal, even dried flower petals to get the colors he needed. Freddie was studying to be a medicine man, and at "sings" or healing ceremonies, he would create the appropriate sandpainting on the earthen floor of a hogan, drizzling the colored sands between thumb and forefinger until the proper religious representation was produced, while chanting special songs to restore harmony and balance to the patient. When the sandpainting was completed and the hypnotic Navajo healing chants had ended, in Navajo tradition, the sandpainting had to be destroyed before dawn. This would avoid any misfortune being inflicted on the singer or the patient.

I rode by quietly while Freddie and Bertha concentrated on their crafts. A few years later their children would perform hoop dances by Dad's store to attract and entertain summer travelers.

Southwest postcard producer, Bob Petley, captured the essence of Freddie and Bertha and their children in a photo he took while in Lupton — Freddie and Bertha in traditional attire, the kids in their hoop dance costumes. That photo was made into a post card and sold in many stores throughout the southwest for years.

Lupton was full of the ordinary and the extraordinary, the simple and the spectacular.

The vast openness around Lupton allowed my imagination to be limitless. Often, people assume living in a remote area creates the kind of isolation that stifles awareness, style, creativity. In fact, it is quite the opposite — it hones instincts. Without limitations, dreams can take shape and solidify. For me, I think being shy made me even more aware and more determined to prove myself.

The world outside our reservation came alive to us through radio. It suggested vivid mental pictures while it brought us news, sports, and lively music. Some evenings, Dad would grab his accordion — he played beautifully — and Mom would tune up her banjo. Together they gave us our own "Grand Ol' Opry," and we joined them in singing songs like *You Are my Sunshine, Let Me Call You Sweetheart,* and *Goodnight, Irene.*

And sometimes on cool summer evenings, we would all sit outside for a concert under a dome of stars that seemed close enough to touch. Dad said the Ortegas had always been musical. One of his sisters had played piano at the silent movies in Holbrook, and one of his brothers taught himself to play the fiddle. It seemed natural, and I felt the musical interest, too. Mom and Dad must have observed how music inspired me, and for my twelfth birthday they bought me a guitar. Mom taught me a few chords. Uncle Earnest, Mom's brother, taught me more chords, and a local Navajo guy, Wilson Clay, worked with me even more. I kept practicing and practicing. My mother encouraged me.

"You can achieve anything you want, if you want it bad enough," she would say.

So I played and practiced and learned country songs like *Nobody's Darlin but Mine,* and *Send Me the Pillow that You Dream On,* and many more. I developed an ear for music and could pick out chords and follow tunes easily. I practiced and practiced. And I sang. And I played.

I never stuttered when I sang. My vocal chords relaxed and I could just sing. Singing helped my confidence, too. My bouts of stuttering lessened dramatically.

Years later, I played guitar with Russell Chamberlain, also. For several years, Russell spent summers in Lupton — as a roadside attraction of sorts — and he would join in our evening jam sessions.

The first time I spotted Russell Chamberlain, he was rambling along Route 66 in a rounded makeshift wooden wagon led by two huge Brahma bulls. I stopped and stared in disbelief, waiting for the wagon to pass by, but it pulled up in front of the store. Out hopped Russell, a man with a huge white mustache, wearing a small brimmed western hat. He looked like a tinker or a snake oil salesman. The bulls stood strong and impressive — each of their long curving horns held a brass ball at the tip — like shining golden knobs.

Russell hopped down and went into the store and he introduced himself to Dad and asked if he could camp there for a few days. I followed as Dad walked outside, while Russell explained that he earned money by charging tourists a dollar, using their own cameras to take a photo with his decorated Brahma bulls. Dad said he could stay on for a few days, which turned into the entire summer. After that Russell came back every summer for years.

Dad considered Russell and his bulls a draw, an attraction, and thought it helped business. Russell helped my guitar playing for sure. After the store closed, on those cool summer evenings, we would sit outside and play guitar together.

After all those years, Russell became part of our summer community. One night, though, a huge summer storm hit Lupton, crashing with thunder and fierce bolts of lightning and sheets of heavy rain. As dawn approached, I strolled outside expecting to inhale the fresh scent of dampened piñon and juniper, but instead an acrid stench permeated the air. Then I saw the bulls laying there, dead.

Russell said they had been struck by lightning. The bulls had both been sizzled. He just stood there staring in disbelief. Later, Russell came into the store to use the phone and gave the operator a number for someone in his family.

He waited there in his wagon — shoulders hunched, looking down — until that family member came to his rescue and hauled him away. He had no reason to spend summers in Lupton ever again.

Unfortunately, Russell Chamberlain had nothing to back up his living. He was dependent on those two Brahma bulls with brass balls on their horns. I knew I didn't want to limit myself to something like that. If I had a store, I would work as hard as I could to build a business — not a roadside attraction.

Boys Will Be *Lupton Boys*

*"Thinking back, we must have been comical customers —
a couple of kids from Lupton with $50, trying to buy a car."*

Long before I was a teenager, Dad had built the gas house, as we called it, a small square block building to store oil, batteries, tires, and such. It was our hangout — when we weren't playing basketball. Of course the only time we weren't playing basketball was when it was dark or snowing. Even the wind didn't stop us. "The Lupton Boys," as we were called around those parts, became a basketball force. And sometimes the force to play basketball outweighed the necessity of watching the gas pumps.

Dad would get so irritated, he would march out of the store and yell, "You guys don't take care of the people; you just play basketball all day. The only time you look is when a pretty girl gets out of a car."

With all that practice, by the time I got to high school, I was a good basketball player. Since Aggie and I were only a year apart, we both played for Sanders High School. Together with the other Navajo players, we had a tough team. We understood one another. Growing up, going to school and playing sports with the Navajos, I learned to think like them.

One time some guys who played basketball for BYU were around the area and heard about "The Lupton Boys." It was arranged for us to play them over at St. Michael's, on the reservation not far from Window Rock. We piled into Armand's car and he drove us over there. St. Michael's Indian School had been founded by the Franciscans at the turn of the century. As the boarding school grew through the years, a high school and gym were added.

We were nervous to play against those college guys, but we had our Lupton guts and rhythm on our side. We ran around them like crazy, Louie Morgan, my brothers Maxie and Aggie, Donald Layton, and me. And we beat them. Like me, I know the others have relived that game over and over again in their minds. It was a great victory.

Though he wasn't on the basketball team, another Navajo that I became great friends with as a high school freshman was Freddie Lynch. He lived on the reservation near Sanders. He had an old car that he drove to school — even though he was only 14 and didn't have a license. One morning as he pulled into the dirt parking lot at the school. I hopped into the car with him, and together we planned an unusual "entrance."

After he parked on a slight incline facing the school and turned off the engine, we slipped out of view, down behind the dashboard, while he put the clutch in and out, forcing the car to roll slowly across the lot — seemingly ghost-driven. Teachers began to yell, and a bunch of kids ran toward the car to stop it. Just then, Freddie and I popped up, and he slammed on the brakes. We thought it was pretty funny, in spite of the fact that we spent most of that morning in the principal's office.

Freddie and I had several other spontaneous high school adventures, especially one summer night in Lupton when we were hanging out in the gas house. There was really no other place to go, so the gas house became the gathering place. Even Clarence Hawthorne, the area's Navajo police officer, stopped there for a rest now and then. His all-night shift was long and boring, and he covered a huge expanse of reservation. That night, Clarence parked the paneled police wagon on the side of the gas house, slid out and yawned and stretched before trudging into the tiny building that housed tires, batteries, and oil.

"It's *tiredness* already," he said, as he tossed his hat onto the table, slid into the beaten-up wooden chair, then put his feet on the table and folded his arms. Within minutes, his eyes closed, his head bobbed, and soon his chin settled on his chest and he was snoring.

Freddie and I gave each other an inspired glance and took a quick look at the sleeping Clarence, knowing he always left the keys in the squad car. Quietly, we darted to the police wagon. The keys were firmly planted in the ignition, and we impulsively decided to drive the police car. I jumped in, put in the clutch and Freddie pushed the wagon until we got down the road, and then I started it. We zipped through the darkness, wondering where to go, so I just kept driving down Route 66 all the way to Gallup and back. We took turns driving, even put on the siren and the lights and raced down the highway like we were in hot pursuit of law breakers. Neither one of us even had a driver's license.

When Clarence woke from his nap and strolled outside, his vehicle was gone. Looking back, it was like a scene out of an episode of Andy Griffith, and Clarence was in a mess that only Barney Fife could understand.

As we got closer to the trading post, I turned the lights off and coasted just out of sight where Clarence stood in front of the gas house. Then we jumped out, ran, and hid.

But Clarence knew we had done it. He didn't want to get himself in trouble either, though, so he kept quiet. But he never left his keys in the ignition again when he stopped by the gas house.

And eventually Freddie Lynch grew up and lost his mischievous edge and settled down. He still lives in Sanders.

In a remote area like ours, transportation was a challenge, and cars were of huge importance to us. Armand continued to drive us to basketball games. But now, Maxie wanted to buy a car. He was getting eager for the freedom a car could provide — and he had all of $50 to buy one. He and Louie Morgan got a ride into Gallup one day, and Maxie did some serious car shopping. He found an old Model T or maybe it was a Model A. Anyway, it was so old, it needed a crank to start it. And it was a really long crank. They took it for a test drive, and the salesman had given them the hard sell and the quick close. But they didn't make a deal. Maxie hesitated to make the $50 offer. He didn't want it to be rejected, so they left.

But, the next day he convinced Louie and me to go back to the Gallup car lot with his $50. Maxie wanted *us* to make the deal. We hiked to Box Canyon and caught the bus to Gallup. Louie sauntered up to the car and I lagged behind. The salesman offered to give us a test drive. We hopped in and after a rattling start with that giant crank, the salesman took us for a spin and told us that buying this car was the opportunity of a lifetime. "Yeah," I muttered, "I can hear it knocking!"

Maxie was convinced we could buy the car for $50 — and after some lengthy discussion, we made the deal. Thinking back, we must have been comical customers — a couple of kids from Lupton with $50, trying to buy a car. But, of course, we weren't buying the most desirable car on the lot, either. And for a 15-year-old kid, I was learning valuable negotiating skills.

Louie had a driver's license. I didn't. He slid behind the wheel and eased the old relic off the lot. No license plates. No insurance. The car chugged uphill, and then it zipped downhill. We sure hoped the mechanical brakes would hold. Louie let me drive part of the way back to Lupton. I maneuvered the wheel with my right hand, and hung my left arm on the open window like I had seen experienced drivers do. When I drove past Box Canyon, I crept along hoping Joe would see me driving, but he didn't. Their store was squeezed so close to the highway, you could almost touch it. I pulled over and stopped past Box Canyon to let Louie drive the rest of the way home. I didn't want Dad to see me driving. I put the old car in neutral, and it sputtered and vibrated while we switched places.

When we pulled up, we saw Maxie pacing outside by the gas pumps, waiting for us. When Dad found out we had bought that car, he was furious.

"You boys, what have you done? You don't even have any insurance," he threw his hands up, exasperated. "You're going to ruin me."

Then he took out after us, and chased us all the way to the Puerco, yelling. He was convinced that car would be nothing but trouble.

Of course, the next morning it had a flat tire. It didn't have a jack, so a strong Navajo neighbor just lifted it up while Maxie and Louie got the tire off, then set it on some blocks until they could repair the tire and change it. Amazingly, that car lasted a long time.

That's when I planned to take machine shop in high school. I knew I would be wanting a car, too, and I knew I'd better know how to take care of one — especially the kind of cars we could afford.

In front of Indian Trails Trading Post in the 1950s in Lupton, Arizona
From left: Gilbert, Joe Upshaw, Max, Jr., Aggie, Jackson Parker, Armand, and Amelia.

Ortega Family, 1956. Back row from left: Aggie, Esther, Armand, Max Jr., Gilbert
Front row from left: Denny, Amelia, Max Sr., Dewey.

Fun in the Fifties

"I was always a little different from most other people, and I wanted to stand out in a way that made me feel like I had something to prove."

Other things about high school began to change, too. The coach at Gallup High School heard what good basketball players Aggie and I were at Sanders. Coach Schlenker observed us in action and recruited us to play for Gallup High. This was unexpected and would be a big change for us — and a great basketball opportunity. Aggie would be a senior, and I would be a junior. Aggie was big, tall, strong.

I was 5'9" and played guard with speed and agility — lightning fast. We were both determined to be assets to the team.

I developed a great relationship with our other coach, Coach Hyson. His son, Dick, a tall guy, played on the team, too, and we became good friends.

Since we were the only two from Lupton attending school in Gallup, we needed transportation, so Dad let us drive the wood-sided station wagon for our daily commute. By then I actually had a license, and Aggie and I would take turns driving the 20 miles to and from Gallup. We became more familiar with Gallup and got to know a lot of people.

On our way to school each day, we drove past the heavy stone buildings that lined the hilly, often muddy, streets of downtown. When Route 66 first opened in 1926, Gallup became a hub for travelers and the center of the Indian arts and crafts business, and later became known as "The Indian Capitol of the World." But it had long before been established as a coal mining and railroad town.

In the 1880s when the railroad pushed west, a payroll office was established along a dusty stretch of tracks. The paymaster's name was David Gallup. When the railroaders headed to the office to pick up their pay, they would say, "I'm going to Gallup." The name stuck.

Things began changing in Gallup in the 1950s. The smell of coal smoke that had permeated the air soon disappeared. The Navajos and Zunis started trading wagons for pickup trucks. The muddy streets had been paved, and the rutted wagon tracks were history. As the town got busier, Basilio DeGregorio relocated and expanded his California Supermarket — even put in a parking lot. The town bustled with business.

Most reservation roads led to Gallup, and Route 66 was Gallup's main street. As it became a busier thoroughfare, it was scheduled to be widened and straightened in McKinley County, which would include the stretch in front of the Atkinson's Box Canyon Trading Post.

This presented a huge problem for Leroy Atkinson, since the Highway Commission discovered that most of his operation sat in the middle of the planned expansion, and he was ordered to remove the encroaching gas pumps and most of the store and restaurant. The store had always hugged the highway, but this had never been a problem before. Well, Leroy was cigar-spitting mad, and he fought and defied the ruling as long as he could. Ultimately, he sold what he could, and the family relocated to Tucson and started over. Sometime earlier Jake and Herman had moved and each opened new highway stores east on Route 66 near Grants, New Mexico.

For me, the '50s were a great time in my life. Not only was basketball going well, but I was still playing guitar and keeping up with current music. Plus, I started a country band — Gil Dean and the Westerners — shortened my first name and used my middle name. There were four members. I played guitar and was lead vocalist. Gilman Yovonavich played fiddle and steel guitar and Bronson Springstead played guitar. Ivan Stearns was the drummer and sometimes, Dick Hyson would sit in on guitar. He sang well also.

We performed mostly country and current '50s music — like Carl Perkins' *Blue Suede Shoes*, some Faron Young, and Elvis. We wrote a few songs, too. But mostly we played popular music. We always dressed in jeans, western shirts, and cowboy boots. My sister, Esther, even made us matching shirts for performances, which gave us a professional look. She was an excellent seamstress. She learned from Mom. When Esther's kids were little, Mom would simply lay one of the kids on top of a piece of butcher paper on the floor, trace around them and create a pattern.

I booked our appearances at high school dances and special events in Gallup. We also performed at several places on the Navajo reservation and at Ramah, just east of Zuni Pueblo, which was 40 miles south of Gallup. But we liked playing in Gallup best, because everyone knew us and it was the most fun. And when I was behind that guitar and singing, my shyness vanished. On stage I blossomed, but I still resisted answering questions in class or speaking in front of a group.

"Gil Dean and the Westerners" began making a name. I was really proud of our band. We were starting to make money, too, and, naturally, I began getting anxious to buy a car.

Soon I found a shiny, black 1950 Mercury that had been customized with Cadillac fins on the back. It had adjustable spotlights like a police car and buttons that opened the doors. That meant that the doors were slick — no handles. The handles had been removed and that area leaded, sanded, primed, and repainted. Near the cowling, close to the windshield wipers, was a hidden button. When punched, it sent a signal to the solenoid, and the door popped open. I liked that. Inside I hung furry black and white dice from the rearview mirror. I thought I had the best car of anyone around, and that was important to me.

I was fun-loving, easy-going — I always had a lot of friends. I guess you'd say I was popular — anyway I had a lot of fun. But, I was always a little different from most other people, and I wanted to stand out in a way that made me feel like I had something to prove.

After school my friends, the guys in the band and Aggie and I, used to meet at the Chocolate Shop. We would buy vanilla cokes, laugh and joke around, talk to girls. The Chocolate Shop was next to Thrifty Drug on Coal Street. Several years later I would have two stores there.

On Friday or Saturday nights, when I was cruising up and down the Gallup streets in my shiny black car, beaming the spotlight at people, sometimes one of my friends would sip on a quart of beer he had in a paper bag. I really didn't drink much, but one night the guys in the band and I were drinking beer a little north of town in the graveyard. The cops came out and found us and threw us in jail — for about an hour — to frighten us, threatening to call our parents. I was scared. I didn't want anyone to ever call my Dad on me. He would have been so mad.

Mom and Dad still expected me to work in the store on weekends and after school when I could. They were never able to see the band play, but they were encouraging and supportive. And they worried about my driving back and forth to Gallup, being only 16 years old. Sometimes, I think they thought it would inhibit me in some way if they attended shows. It's not like they didn't want to see me play. It was more about letting go — allowing me to do it my own way — an acceptance of the person I had chosen to become. I see now how important that was to my personal development.

The band and basketball were all I truly cared about. School didn't interest me much, but I managed to graduate with a B average. Actually, my nonchalant attitude toward school got me voted "least likely to succeed." Least likely to succeed — what an inspiration!

After graduation, the band took on more importance. I dreamed of recording, going to Nashville. But as reality began to set in, I knew it would take the kind of money I couldn't come up with, not yet anyway. The band's local popularity continued. Actually, we were busier after graduation and stayed together about two more years. I still helped Dad in the store and even got a job at the Inspection Station for a while. But that didn't last. I never pictured myself working at the Inspection Station. Thoughts of business and the desire for my own store began surfacing in my imagination. But, for now, I put all my energy into the band.

One morning Bronson and I were driving through town to make arrangements for a performance, when I spotted a pretty girl walking to school with Bronson's sister.

"Who is that girl with Loralynn?" I asked Bronson.

"Linda VanderWagen," he answered. As I pried more information out of him, he told me that her dad was a trader in Zuni. She lived on a ranch south of Gallup with her dad sometimes, or in town with her mom, since her parents had separated. Her mom was a proofreader for the *Gallup Independent*, the local newspaper.

"Well, I hope they want a ride to school," I said as I turned the car around quickly and zoomed up just ahead of the girls and stopped. A small bout of shyness hit, so I made Bronson stick his head out the window and offer them a ride. They both ran to the car and jumped in. Bronson introduced Linda to me, but she said she knew who I was from the band. She was even prettier than I first thought. Her long hair fell off her shoulders in soft curls, and she had sparkling hazel eyes and a great smile. She seemed cheerful and vivacious. We talked and laughed, and I drove around the block an extra time before dropping the girls off at school. Bronson said later that his sister told him that Linda liked me, but figured she probably didn't have a chance because lots of girls liked me. She said I had an Elvis look.

A few weeks later when "Gil Dean and the Westerners" played at the L-Bar-E Rodeo in Ramah, just east of Zuni, I saw Linda again, talking to a guy there. I felt a twinge of jealousy. She was so pretty, and her chic cowgirl style showed off her cute figure. During our break, I wandered over to her and asked her to sit with me — and she did. After the break, we did an Elvis tune,

"That's All Right, Mama," and the crowd went wild. Then I sang one directed at Linda.

Our romance blossomed. Linda went to almost all of our performances and watched me play and sing. And I liked to pick her up after school in the afternoon. I'd cruise the school a little early and park on the hill across from her classroom, then rev up the engine so the souped-up muffler would send her a signal. I knew she was looking out of the classroom window at me. From that hilltop spot, I could see downtown where solid stone buildings lined the streets and ahead of me the El Rancho Hotel and Route 66, and across to the railroad tracks and beyond into the desolate reservation landscape to the north. Sometimes Gallup appeared gray and colorless, especially in the winter when the town was seized by snow. After the snow melted, the streets oozed with mud tracked in from the dirt roads of the reservation.

While I parked and waited for Linda to get out of class, I sank down behind the steering wheel and read Richie Rich comic books. I could see myself like Richie Rich, driving a Rolls Royce, living in a big house. But, of course, I had to find a way to earn this, since I wouldn't be inheriting the elegance of his "Lord Fauntleroy" life. Still, I would stare into the trappings of his wealth and I would dream. I wanted to make money. And I wasn't afraid of what it would take to get it, or how hard I would have to work. I knew nobody was going to chauffeur me into such a life. Even though I was still helping Dad in the store, he couldn't support all of us much longer. Sometimes I wondered why he was satisfied with his business and didn't want it to grow. He had been offered other locations on the highway for practically nothing. The thought of that potential gave me an energy surge. I would have taken those opportunities and run with them. Armand would have, too.

But, at that time, the important things for me were the band and Linda.

After school, I would take Linda and her friends to the Chocolate Shop. I made sure I always picked up the check for the cokes or sodas or malts — whatever they wanted. Then I would take her home. Since her parents were separated, sometimes she stayed in town with her mom, Grace, or with her dad, Bernie, at the ranch in VanderWagen, about halfway to Zuni. And sometimes her parents switched from one place to the other, according to necessity.

Bernie had a trading post in the center of Zuni where, like Dad, he sold staples — and bought beautiful Zuni jewelry, which, like Dad, he sold to tourists. I enjoyed being in his store. Understanding how the business worked made the store and Zuni come to life for me.

Zuni was a quaint, historic community. Unlike the Navajos who were spread out over a vast reservation, Pueblo Indians, like the Zunis, lived within a community setting. Squat stone houses surrounded the traditional plaza, each with an adobe *horno* outside for baking thick, crusty Pueblo bread. Inside their simple dwellings, most had an area for jewelry making where the craftsmen produced handmade sterling pieces with intricate inlay and fine stone-cut settings in thin needlepoint-shaped turquoise, and tiny circular petitpoint.

I appreciated being there for some of the ceremonies and dances, too, especially "Shalako." Held next to the river when the new moon arrived during the winter solstice, six dancers – who represented the gods – captured everyone's attention. The Shalako effigies, which are about eight feet high, are attached to a pole and covered by a long white cotton garment bordered in symbolic reds and greens. From within the garment, the personator supports the pole attached to his belt. An opening in the cloth allows him to see. The impressive head or mask of the Shalako is crowned with a ruff of eagle feathers, has staring eyes, a long tubular mouth, and horns that curve up from either side of the cheeks, and a thick ruffle of feathers around the neck. The Shalako ceremony lasted all day and all night.

In the morning the tall gods would move swiftly toward the river where they each planted a feathered prayer stick into designated spots in the earth. That day everyone, especially the children, gathered around the plaza for *"Giveaway."* Like the other residents of the Zuni plaza, Linda and I stood on the roof of her dad's store and tossed down fruit and candy to the lively crowd below. Participating in *Giveaway* was fun.

The Navajos would bestow gifts on those who attended a *Kinaalda* — a young woman's coming-of-age ceremony — but in those days it was taboo for non-Navajos to attend. The Navajos also held Squaw Dances and Fire Dances, and powerful healing ceremonies. Sometimes we would watch a squaw dance from the dark distance and observe the silhouettes of dancers around the huge bonfire, where couples danced a two-step to the rhythm of the Navajo singer and the beat of his drum. The Squaw Dance, *Nadaa'*, as it was properly called, gave people of these remote communities an opportunity to socialize.

As Linda and I continued dating, our romance became more serious. Later that year, we got married. I was 21 and she was 16. I thought Linda was the prettiest, sweetest girl I had ever known, and she was enthusiastic and adventurous. She believed in me and was willing to go anywhere to follow me and my dreams, and we wanted to work together. Linda was the only girl

I knew who could understand and talk about business — ultimately, my favorite topic of conversation.

Even though I still had dreams of going to Nashville and recording, reality struck. And so did opportunity. Armand asked me to come and work for him in Gage, New Mexico. He would teach me the business.

Well, it looked like everything was falling into place for me. "In place." Right. Like a long row of dominos, teetering on edge.

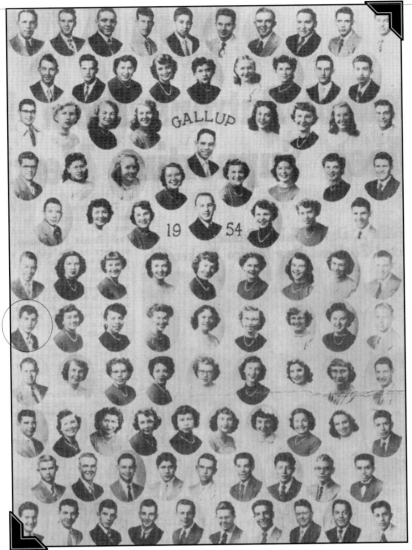

Gilbert's high school graduating class 1954.

Gilbert worked at the Arizona Inspection Station for a short time after high school.

Gilbert played basketball at Gallup High, 1953-54.

Gilbert Ortega
Guard

Gilbert and Linda at Linda's mother's house in Gallup,1956.

Gilbert and Linda's wedding photo, May 22, 1957
Truth or Consequences, New Mexico.

Training Post

*"I was ready to advance, and I knew Armand was a good teacher.
I felt like I was on scholarship to the Harvard of the Highway."*

Armand had married a few years earlier and recently bought a store from Jake Atkinson along the highway in southern New Mexico, near Deming. Armand was determined to strike out on his own, and Jake had sold him the location. Everybody on the highway was used to "creative financing," so Jake and Armand made some payment arrangements. In a strange way, all the traders created their own economy — with each other, with the Navajos, with the vendors, always figuring how to buy, sell, trade.

Jake moved on to Tucson and opened a business there, joining his brother Leroy who had already opened Indian Village on a busy downtown corner. Herman still had his Cobra Garden near Grants — a regular roadside attraction. Snakes were the big thing back then.

The big thing for me, though, was getting married and going to work for Armand. He wanted us in Gage right away.

My car was packed with our few belongings, and we headed down the highway — two kids starting a new life — and me, starting a career, hopefully. We didn't have time for a wedding in town, so Linda's mom, Grace, came with us and we stopped in Truth or Consequences, New Mexico, and got married by a Justice of the Peace. Since I didn't have a ring, Grace gave Linda her own wedding band to wear. It took 12 years before I could buy her a diamond, and Linda said it took just about that long for Grace to regard me as a gem.

Gage, New Mexico, was a flat, open and desolate spot about 20 miles east of Deming along Highway 80, which is now Interstate 10, the highway that stretches across southern New Mexico with El Paso, Texas, to the east and Tucson, Arizona, to the west. It was late spring when we arrived, and the desert around Gage was scruffy, dry and filled with rattlesnakes. Several inviting highway signs led us to the store, which was easy to see from the highway — and it sat on the north side, the best location. The building displayed the familiar highway architecture — rectangular — long across the front, giving it good visibility from the highway. Apache Village Trading Post was brightly painted and advertised cheap gasoline, as well as the snack bar with its home-made cherry cider and delicious milk shakes and, of course, Indian jewelry, crafts and gifts.

Armand worked hard buying merchandise on credit where he could — trying to turn inventory and generate cash flow, building his business. He had brought Benny Upshaw from Lupton and our Aunt Margie to sell in the store and then hired a couple of local guys to run the snack bar and help with maintenance. Linda would work in the snack bar and the store, as well. And I wanted to work compulsively — wanted to learn the next level of business.

When we pulled in, I recognized everyone's cars parked out front. We had started parking in front years ago in Lupton, so it looked like we had a lot of customers inside — it encouraged more tourists to stop.

I was anxious to get started. Armand became my teacher and mentor. I became his best student.

Home for my bride and me was a tiny trailer — more like a camping trailer — that sat behind the store so close to the railroad tracks that, when the trains would rumble and roar past there at night, they would rock that little trailer. We had running water, just cold at first from a hose Armand hooked to the trailer, but no bathroom. We had to shower and use the restroom inside Armand and Marie's quarters, which were connected to the store. Linda was accustomed to better living conditions, but she was a good sport.

Armand spent all of his time working, improving the store. Marie was busy with their children running in and out of the store. She couldn't let them play outside in the late spring, because there were too many rat-tlesnakes. Having grown up on a farm in Louisiana, then graduating from nursing school, Marie had adventurously taken a nursing job on the Navajo reservation at St. Michael's. That's where she met Armand. Now transplanted in Gage, she had adapted well, set up a home for her growing family, and even planted a garden.

I was ready to advance, and I knew Armand was a good teacher. I felt like I was on scholarship to the "Harvard of the Highway." I absorbed myself in the business. This is where I learned the difference between profit and loss, got my education. And I learned about hard work, too. No 40-hour week in this business. I put in seven days a week, 12 hours a day. I took a day off now and then, but that was it.

I was ready for this, powered by nervous energy, enthusiasm, and a desire to make money. I learned which suppliers to buy from, how to get quantity price breaks, how to take proper markups for profit and sales, and how to arrange merchandise attractively. I watched what sold the quickest and kept track of back stock. Running out of a hot seller would be a cash-flow crime.

When figuring the markup on merchandise, Armand would shrug his shoulders, then put his cigarette down so he could emphasize his theory, like a retail scholar.

"You have to figure in the lights, the gas, the shoe polish, the toilet paper," he would repeat with a snap of his fingers. "Light bulbs, stamps, and so on … that's the only way you'll ever make any money. And you have to learn the percentages."

On the highway, I already knew the basic needs of travelers were gasoline and restrooms. Impulsive purchases, like curios and jewelry depended on clever merchandising and competitive pricing.

Hunger and thirst also motivated customers to pull off the highway, and the snack bar at the back of the trading post served juicy hamburgers, french fries, and milk shakes. We also made and sold hundreds of gallon jugs of cherry cider. We knew the longer the customers lingered in the store, the more merchandise we were likely to show them — and the more money they were likely to spend.

And then there was the Snake House.

As if there weren't enough rattlesnakes slithering around the desert, tourists paid 50 cents each to get into the Snake House. Through a set of double doors and to the left stood a huge, glass-enclosed cage — the dwelling of the 18-foot python. Cobras and more rattlers slid around in the adjoining cages. We fed the python live rabbits and chickens and watched him swallow his prey whole, then pass along lump by lump as the snake digested it. We didn't have a lot of entertainment in Gage.

Besides, snakes were the roadside craze then. The Snake House was there when Armand bought the store, but he added to it by purchasing the python, some cobras, and even a few Gila monsters from Herman Atkinson's Cobra Gardens near Grants, New Mexico. There were also guys who came around selling rattlesnakes in the spring. But these snakes would die off, and we had to get new ones. It was important to have some attraction to lure people off the highway — snakes worked like a charm.

Then one day the python squeezed out of its cage. Armand spotted it first. We were frozen in a simultaneous shudder, and we had no idea how it had happened. Fortunately, there were no customers in the store at the time. We knew we had to get that python back in its cage — and quickly. It took all of us to lift the huge, scaly, squirming mass back into his cage. It was like wrestling with a giant twisting tree trunk.

After that, we watched the Snake House with spine-tingling suspense and made it even more secure. But we still worried. What if there was a fire and all the snakes got out? What if one of the cobras squirmed out of its cage and bit someone? Armand and I went to Deming and talked to a doctor who said he would order anti-venom and keep it in his office. If any bites occurred, we were to call and meet him halfway with the victim and he would administer the anti-venom. Later we wondered why he didn't just teach Marie how to give the anti-venom. She was a nurse.

Fortunately, we never had an incident.

Whenever Armand and I went down the highway to Deming, we would stop for lunch or coffee and talk business, and scribble projections on napkins — our answer to the pro forma. Somehow, we would always meet up with Carl Kempton, a fair-haired 15-year-old who did odd jobs around town. He seemed like an enthusiastic hard-worker, and he had an irresistible smile. Armand and I had a good feeling about him — we were good judges of people. We offered Carl a job handling the Snake House. On a napkin I wrote $5.00 a day, plus meals. A hungry teenager, Carl agreed.

Carl made sure the python never got out again, or any other snakes either. I was impressed with how quickly he caught on to the workings of the business, and he could fix anything around the store. He was a fast learner, and he fit in like a member of the family. A few weeks after he started working, I strolled by the snack bar, and saw Carl sitting there tossing down french fries and munching on his second burger. I knew he was content with our agreement. Within earshot of Carl I told Armand, "You know the only mistake we made with Carl was letting him eat whatever he wants. He's going to break us."

Everyone laughed, and Carl just gave us a toothy grin and popped a handful of fries into his mouth.

We had a congenial crew. Linda worked in the snack bar and in the store, too. She was always smiling. Sometimes I thought maybe she smiled at some other guy and I would get jealous. But she reassured me, said she couldn't help it, she just smiled a lot. Linda developed a great friendship with Margie, and they would spend evenings together in our trailer, talking and laughing while I worked. Poor Linda, she was only 16. There was nothing fun for her to do. She couldn't get dressed up and go out to dinner or dancing, go to a movie. She would have liked to have been around other couples our age, I'm sure. I worked day and night. She was stuck out in the middle of nowhere. And she was expecting our first child.

Linda also developed a close bond with Marie — she was easy to talk to and gave Linda sound advice. Their big outing was to drive to Deming to buy groceries. Marie and the kids would hop into the car and Linda would always drive, because Marie never learned to drive.

I knew I didn't pay enough attention to Linda. I thought she began to understand that business had to come first.

"You work until 9:00 or 10:00 o'clock every night, Gilbert," she would complain. "I spend my evenings sitting at this trailer window watching the rats eat the corn in Marie's garden."

I would look around that little trailer, ashamed that it was the only home I could provide. And here she was, expecting our first child. I didn't know what to say.

But nothing changed.

Gayle Dean was born a few months later. She was a beautiful baby and Linda managed to create a mini-nursery in the trailer.

It was in 1958, during our first year there, that Armand bought a store in Tucson from Leroy Atkinson, and he and Marie and Armand, Jr., Larry, Amelia and Billy moved to Tucson. Armand was confident that I could run Apache Village Trading Post myself. I was ready.

This meant we could move into the living quarters behind the store. Linda wanted to paint the bedroom for the baby, but there was no extra money for paint. A few mornings later, Uncle Eppie, Mom's brother-in-law, stopped by for coffee. He worked for the highway department and would drop by often. He gave us a can of the paint they used for highway stripes — that bright yellow paint. Obviously, it wasn't the color Linda had envisioned for her nursery, but she and Margie painted the bedroom. To me the walls looked like highway signs, and that's what I used the remaining paint for — more highway signs.

And it's a good thing we had more living space, because our second daughter, Desirée, was born — less than a year after Gayle Dean. She looked like Linda's baby picture. Linda ran between the store and the babies.

By the time we celebrated Gayle Dean's first birthday, we were getting concerned because she still wasn't walking. We took her to several doctors in Deming, in Albuquerque — to different hospitals. Finally, she was diagnosed with non-progressive, localized muscular dystrophy, in her hip joints. This meant that she would learn to walk, but it would always be a struggle. I would have given anything to see her run and jump. I tried to imagine how much it would have hurt me if I hadn't been able to play basketball. For years I tried to find a therapy or cure. But none was discovered. Gayle learned to live with it and accept it. I always wished I could have changed things for her. Even now, I would give up everything for her mobility.

I wasn't the kind of dad to help change diapers or feed bottles to the babies. Instead, I made them laugh and got them excited.

I worked and worked and worked. Sometimes I didn't even want to stop for lunch, so I'd grab a strawberry soda pop and toss in some peanuts, like when I was a kid, or down a Coke and a candy bar. I marked merchandise until late in the evening and filled displays. We were doing more business, and that satisfied me.

But things were changing in our marriage. Linda and I fought a lot. She would say she was leaving. "Leave the kids with me," I would threaten, hoping that would make her stay. Sometimes she would grab Gayle and Desirée up in her arms and clutch onto them and hike along the railroad tracks, like she was trying to run away — maybe she was hoping a train would come along and pick her up. I would tear out of the store and run next to the tracks and make her come back.

She said she had expected our marriage to be special, that I would cherish her. But she knew that the business would always be more important, and that hurt her. All I wanted was for her to accept me for who I was and what I wanted to become — to know that someday I would be successful. Someday.

But after three years of marriage, she left me. She took the kids and went to Gallup to live with her mother. I didn't want her to leave, and I was torn into a million pieces. I had never felt that kind of hurt. I agonized over it. I couldn't even think straight or sleep. My mind and body hung in limbo. Even though I tried to understand Linda, I didn't know what to say or do. And it didn't help that Gage was the pit of the southwest. I couldn't blame her. But it was devastating; it almost killed me, and took me years to get over.

I couldn't stay there anymore — alone.

Fortunately, Armand had a new opportunity for me in Tucson, and he recruited Maxie to take over at Gage. Maxie, his wife, Mildred, and their two children, Max III and Debra, moved from Lupton to Gage.

In 1957, Gilbert went to Armand's Apache Village Trading Post near Deming, New Mexico to learn the next level of the business.

Grandmothers come to visit
From left: Amelia, Gayle Dean, Desireé,
Grace, 1959 in Gage.

Gilbert, 22, in the trading post cafe in
Gage, New Mexico.

GALLUP VISITORS this weekend are Mr. and Mrs. Gilbert Ortega and daughter
Gayle Dean from Deming, N, Mex. Mrs. Ortega is the former Linda VanderWagen of
Zuni, daughter of Mr. and Mrs. B. J. VanderWagen. Ortega is the son of Mr. and
Mrs. Max Ortega of Lupton, Arizona.
Monday, January 13, 1958, as appeared in the Gallup Independent

Tucson Trials & Tribulations

"Because I was dejected and so unhappy, I worked longer and harder."

With renewed hope, I moved to Tucson. Driving towards "The Old Pueblo," I peered into an endless turquoise sky that held an occasional cloud, like a puffy cotton ball tossed into the air. From the Benson highway, even in 1960, Tucson looked like a big city — compared to Gage and Deming. I scanned the red-brick structures of the University of Arizona campus, then glanced toward the tall buildings of downtown, where I was headed. The outskirts of the Sonoran desert town were spread with tall stately saguaros, fragrant creosote bush and thorny cholla and prickly pear cactus, with the towering Catalina mountains as a backdrop. I hoped the desert town would be a welcome change.

I had arranged to lease the jewelry department at Indian Village, Armand's downtown store, which he had bought from Leroy Atkinson. The store was located on the corner of Congress and Scott, down the street from the post office. As I drove through downtown, along Pennington Street, past Jacome's and Levy's department stores, I saw the tall and impressive Valley National Bank building, then continued driving around downtown until I spotted Indian Village and parked in front of the five-and-ten-cent-store across the street.

Anxious to get started, I went to work right away. I absorbed myself in the store, especially the jewelry department. Armand counted on me to run things for him there, because he had opened another Indian Village in the Wilmot Plaza shopping center, on the corner of Speedway and Wilmot — what was then the far east side of town. Leroy was still in business in Tucson and so was Jake.

Our tourist season there was winter, and downtown was still a draw, especially during the Rodeo Parade, the last Thursday in February. It seemed like everyone who lived there, or was visiting, crowded the streets. In Tucson tradition, all the entries were completely horse-drawn, and local high school bands marched and played spirited tunes — a regular Tucson holiday. That event brought us a lot of business.

Because I was dejected and so unhappy, I worked longer and harder. Even though business was good in downtown Tucson, the rents were really high — we were paying $2,000 a month for 1500 square feet in 1960. Sometimes we would pay the rent with postdated checks, hoping sales and cash flow would catch up with the overhead. And, in reality, shopping centers were taking business away from downtown. I worked constantly trying to build the business and trying not to think about Linda.

Emotionally, I was miserable and wanted things to be different. I needed an escape. That's when I got hooked on diet pills — amphetamines. For about six months, amphetamines powered my life. I thought I could do no wrong. Invincible, I could work forever. Sometimes after work, I would drive to Gallup and see Linda and the kids at her mother's house, then turn around and go back to Tucson and work again. I kept trying to convince her to come back.

Armand recognized what was happening with the amphetamines and confronted me.

"You've got to stop that stuff, Gilbert," he demanded.

I told him I was climbing the walls. I never slept.

"You're skin and bones," he told me. "Those pills are taking their toll on you."

Finally, I got delirious and sick. I knew I had to quit and finally I did. I swore I would never try any other drugs after what happened to me with those diet pills.

I convinced Linda to come back, and we rented a small two-bedroom house near Wilmot, a few blocks from where Armand had bought a home. We didn't have to live behind the store, and the kids could even go swimming at Armand and Marie's house. That was the first time they had ever seen a swimming pool.

Tucson was a welcome environment, and I was happy to have my family back. I tickled and teased the girls, and would pick them up by their jeans and fly them around. They seemed happy, too. Linda would take Marie and her kids and Gayle Dean and Desirée on picnics to Sabino Canyon or Mt. Lemmon. They would drive up the winding road to the top where, at over 9,000 ft., dense forests of ponderosa pines offered cool summer picnicking. And sometimes Grace would come to visit us and bring my mom with her.

There were a lot of nice things about Tucson, but there just wasn't enough business and the rents downtown took their toll. That location was doomed. There was no way we could catch up to the overhead. They closed us up — locked us out.

And to make matters worse, I-10 bypassed the store in Gage. So Apache Village Trading Post was history, too.

But Armand was very sharp — a survivor. He always said, "Whatever happens, they can't kill you." And he kept going. He was right. You can't allow yourself to assume victim status. You have to keep going.

We concentrated on the Wilmot Plaza store, and we needed an attraction to get more business. So, Armand had Freddie Stevens come down from Lupton and create sandpaintings on a platform in the front window of the store. There, Freddie, part medicine man and part showman, became a hit. Dressed in a traditional Navajo velvet tunic worn over his slacks, with a silver concho belt encircling his waist, he sat with legs tucked under him, well-worn Kaibab moccasins peeking out from under his slacks. People were fascinated, watching him drizzle colored sand through his thumb and forefinger to create a healing image, something most had never seen.

When a customer approached him and asked how he had learned to do that, he replied, "Correspondence course. Ten easy lessons," in his clipped Navajo accent, then chuckled. He never tried to impress anyone by saying he was a medicine man. Freddie would work all day, then, in Navajo tradition, destroy the sandpainting just before we closed the store in the evening. Eventually, he created some sandpaintings that weren't sacred quality and could be left in the window. Freddie became an attraction. Even Ray Manley, Tucson's premier photographer of *Arizona Highways* status, took photos of Freddie at work.

In 1960, Gilbert went to Tucson to run the jewelry department of Armand's Indian Village Trading Post.

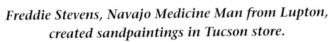

Freddie Stevens, Navajo Medicine Man from Lupton, created sandpaintings in Tucson store.

The School of Hard Knocks

"I think sometimes people actually get happy when bad things happen to someone else. And that is really sad."

Tucson couldn't support all of us, and I was anxious to try it on my own, though I didn't know where to turn. Linda and I moved back to Gallup, where we had to live with Linda's mother. I never thought I would end up living with my mother-in-law. Soon Gilbert, Jr. was born. He looked like my baby picture and my dad's.

Money was an endless problem. Linda worked part-time in a shoe store in Gallup to make ends meet. Grace helped with the kids.

By then Leroy Atkinson was back in Gallup. Tucson was a tough town for business, and it hadn't paid off for Leroy either. He had opened a couple of stores in Gallup. One was a small location called "Many Goats Trading Post" and Leroy agreed to sell it to me for $3,000. Of course, I didn't have $3,000, so Leroy accepted payments. I guess we created our own economy between the Ortegas and the Atkinsons. Besides, he probably felt bad about the Congress and Scott store in Tucson being closed down. That was the store Armand had bought from him. We were all struggling then, but we trusted each other.

I worked and worked, and learned more about the jewelry business. Gallup was definitely the place to broaden my knowledge of Indian jewelry. It was the heart of the Indian arts and crafts business.

Since Gage was in the history books, Aunt Margie came back to Gallup and helped in the store. So did my cousin Frances. Later I sold this store to my brother Aggie.

I was always looking for a fresh opportunity, so when I heard the buzz about a sawmill operation being created on the reservation in an area named Navajo, I found out everything I could to see if there was any business potential.

This spot called Navajo was just north of Window Rock where the Chuska Mountains rose high above the vast reservation plateau, abundant with dense alpine forests. For many years the ponderosa pines had been the source of building materials for the Navajos — using only what they needed. But, on the advice of the Bureau of Indian Affairs, it was decided that the tribe should open a sawmill in the town of Navajo. Between logging and lumber operations, a productive business was envisioned in the 500,000 acre forest. It was estimated that the Navajo Forest Products Industries would employ 400 Navajo workers, who would live there in company housing.

When I heard about the venture, I knew it had opportunity written all over it. Those workers would need groceries, gas, household items. I developed a plan and approached the tribal council in Window Rock with a proposal.

After I presented my proposal and explained the business plan, they agreed to lease me the land at Red Lake, next to Navajo. But first I had to get an Indian Trader's license from the tribe in Window Rock. Since anyone who did business on reservation property had to be a licensed Indian trader, and licensing requires government approval, it often takes time. But because they knew me and my family, they didn't have to do an extensive background check.

With my Indian Trader's license, I was able to begin building Red Lake Shopping Center. As part of my business agreement, I would pay the Navajo tribe a percentage of the gross sales.

As proposed to the tribe, Red Lake Shopping Center would be a 7,000 square foot store with gas pumps out front. The store would serve the daily needs of the developing community and workforce. None of the planned housing had been constructed yet, and the Navajo workers commuted from the nearby reservation.

The plan lacked one ingredient — money and manpower.

I convinced Carl Kempton to help me. Carl was living in Lupton after the Gage store was bypassed and had become part of the family. Carl was diverse and capable. He could do construction and electrical work, as well as merchandise and manage a store. He had learned it all. And at Red Lake Carl worked 12 to 16 hours a day.

When vendors and investors looked at the plan, most were impressed with the potential. So, from several different individuals, I received commitments for building materials, goods and merchandise. Carl's parents loaned me $3,500.

It took almost a year to build and complete everything, to merchandise the store and get it opened. I had to wholesale jewelry on the road and work at Dad's to get extra cash. Leroy Atkinson helped me again. We were all broke at that time. He was going out of the retail business in Gallup and had decided to go back into jewelry, hiring silversmiths, and wholesaling the jewelry. He gave me his old fixtures, tables, and remaining dry goods, as well as some clothing in two sizes — extra large and extra small.

Carl and I stocked the new store with groceries, dry goods, and a selection of household items. Many of the same suppliers Dad had dealt with gave me credit.

Red Lake was an instant success. Finally, I was seeing some money — a good cash flow. This was the break I needed. To encourage business, I offered to cash the paychecks for the employees at the sawmill. But, naturally, this presented a huge cash shortage problem.

I could get the bank to advance me only $5,000 to cash paychecks but I was able to raise another $3-4,000. To cash checks for 400 employees at $100 each would add up to $40,000 a week. However, I knew that the more checks I cashed, the more merchandise I would sell. So then I figured out how to cash them all. For example, if the check was for $100 and they spent $20 in the store, I would give them my own business check for $80. That way they could cash the check in Gallup with one of the traders over the weekend. And I made sure that I was at the bank by 9 a.m. Monday to deposit all the tribal checks. This seemed to be working, and the cash flow was gaining momentum, with all the profits going back into building inventory.

I couldn't have done it without Carl. He was a real asset. He lived in a trailer behind the store. I still lived in Gallup with Linda and the kids at her mother's house. Maybe now I could afford another place to live. Besides, we had another baby on the way.

Then disaster struck. Only 30 days after it opened, Red Lake burned to the ground.

Carl woke to the roar of the blaze around 2 a.m., and called me immediately. I raced there from Gallup along the dark stretch of reservation roads. Carl tried to control the blaze, but the wind swirled and whipped around and fed the flames. He ran into the store and threw things out in a futile effort to save something from the blaze. In the 30 minutes it took me to race over the the deserted roads, toward the huge cloud of smoke that broke through the darkness ahead of the Chuska Mountains, the fire had consumed everything. When I arrived, nothing was left but a pile of smoldering ash — and the beginning of a nightmare.

It had been impossible to control the blaze. There wasn't even a fire extinguisher. The closest fire department was 50-75 miles away. I had no insurance. Everything was gone. I owed everyone.

I was so sick I didn't know what to do. I was frozen in despair. I felt like ending it all.

Eventually I got hold of my senses and knew I had to deal with it. What should I do? File bankruptcy? I didn't know which road to take. I heard Armand's wise words ringing in my ears, "They can't kill you." Now I knew what that meant.

I drove to Red Lake and wandered around through the rubble looking for a clue. There were no investigators to identify the cause of the fire. The tribe didn't investigate anything. I wracked my brain. I searched for signs. There was no way of knowing what had caused the fire. There were no answers, only questions and speculation. I would never know. All that hard work and potential had literally gone up in smoke.

It seemed like everything was against me.

But I was young — only about 25. Looking back, I didn't know what I was doing. I just did it. It seemed like people didn't want me to succeed, either, and I was convinced that some were secretly happy that Red Lake had burned down. They thought I was too young to make it. I think sometimes people actually get happy when bad things happen to someone else. And that is really sad.

I decided that I couldn't go bankrupt. I had to be strong. I felt responsible to the people who had gone out of their way to get me started. So, I vowed to pay everybody back. I just didn't know how — or when.

I learned a lot from Red Lake.

Empty Pockets, Big Dreams

*"My God, where am I going from here? I'm better than this.
What's going to happen to me?"*

After Red Lake burned down, I had no money. My car was repossessed. I was flat broke, and I lost faith in myself. Linda lost faith in me, too.

I felt butchered. I was so broke, I couldn't even buy bread and milk for our kids — Renée had just been born, and I felt guilty bringing that beautiful baby into my shattered world.

And Linda had had it with me, I guess. Poor Linda, she was only 21 — with four small kids.

"Why don't you go to a gas station and get a job pumping gas or something?" she pleaded. "Get a job, please. Anything."

Her words tore into me like a fresh wound. So that was it; she thought all I was capable of doing was just pumping gas, like I did when I was a kid at Lupton.

Things were so bad that a few days later, Linda's mother kicked me out of her house. I wondered if Linda had encouraged her.

When I left, I felt completely hopeless.

Carl loaned me an old 1950 Mercury, and I parked it in an alley in Gallup at night and slept in the car for about a week—hiding out. I was too humiliated to go back to Lupton just yet and let anyone know that Grace had kicked me out. Mom and Dad felt bad enough about Red Lake.

But I needed money, and thought if I went to Tucson, I could borrow some from Armand. So I drove Carl's car to Lupton. Since Carl's car probably wouldn't make it to Tucson, I talked to Maxie, but still didn't tell my parents that Linda's mother had kicked me out. Maxie said I could use his old Lincoln to go to Tucson.

After Red Lake, Mom must have sensed that my desperation was building and hunted for a poem she had cut out of a magazine and saved for me. She hoped it would inspire me to keep trying, rebuild my desire to succeed.

She gave me the poem. I put it in my wallet and kept it there, and read it often — sometimes just staring at it trying to believe in the possibilities it suggested. There were times when it was the only thing in my wallet.

Don't Quit

When things go wrong, as they sometimes will,
When the road you're trudging seems all uphill,
When the funds are low and the debts are high,
And you want to smile, but you have to sigh,
When care is pressing you down a bit —
Rest if you must, but don't you quit.

Life is queer with its twists and turns,
As every one of us sometimes learns,
And many a fellow turns about
When he might have won had he stuck it out.
Don't give up though the pace seems slow—
You may succeed with another blow.

Often the goal is nearer than
It seems to a faint and faltering man;
Often the struggler has given up
When he might have captured the victor's cup;
And he learned too late when the night came down,
How close he was to the golden crown.

Success is failure turned inside out—
The silver tint of the clouds of doubt,
And you never can tell how close you are,
It may be near when it seems afar;
So stick to the fight when you're hardest hit, —
It's when things seem worst that you mustn't quit.

– Anonymous

I sat out by the gas pumps and read the poem. I wanted to believe it. I wanted to believe in myself again.

Maxie gave me the keys to his car. It was parked in front of the store. I thanked him and went back in and said goodbye to Mom and Dad. I needed to get down the road to Tucson and see Armand. Still I didn't reveal my desperation.

The car had some gas in it, and I had $3.00 left in my pocket. I would need more gas. And I was getting hungry. By the time I stopped in Winslow and put $2.50 worth of gas in the car, I was starving. With the 50 cents I had left, I bought a bottle of catsup at a nearby store, where I also snatched four slices of bread out of a loaf on the shelf and slipped them inside my shirt. I couldn't believe I had resorted to stealing bread. When I got into the car, I squeezed a big glob of catsup on each of the slices of white bread, then quickly slapped them together — two juicy catsup sandwiches. After I swallowed the sandwiches, I stopped at another gas station and drank a bunch of water so I felt full.

I didn't know what to do any more. Sometimes I just felt like crying. I was at a point where I thought, "My God, where am I going from here? I'm better than this. What's going to happen to me?" As the car hummed along, some of my despair seemed to lift. Maybe the open road helped. I thought about the poem Mom had given me, and somehow I knew I couldn't quit. I needed a plan. An "empty pocket" plan.

Then, just outside of Tucson, the car began bumping and pulling. The right rear tire had blown out.

I screeched to the side of the highway, jumped out of the car. When I ran and popped the trunk to grab the jack and the spare, I became furious.

"Dammit, Maxie," I yelled into the trunk.

"There's no spare tire. What the hell am I supposed to do now?"

Angry, I grabbed the jack, and when I had it in place and the car was jacked up, I loosened the lug nuts, pulled the flat tire off and rolled it along the highway, hoping a gas station would miraculously appear.

The late afternoon sun beat down on me. I was thirsty, hungry, and disgusted. Where was I going to get money to patch the tire? If I could find a station, maybe they would let me use their phone to call Armand.

I rolled the tire and swore. Rolled the tire. Swore some more. A long stretch of road and desert was all I saw ahead of me. I stared down at my beat-up cowboy boots, watching more dust accumulate on the stitching with each step.

A car pulling a trailer heading north from Tucson slowed and pulled off on the other side of the road, and the driver rolled down his window.

"Hey, Gilbert, what do you have to sell?" he yelled to me.

Surprised, I lifted my head and turned quickly and stared into a small miracle.

"Jimmy Silva! Boy, am I glad to see you."

Jimmy swung his vehicle around and stopped next to where I stood holding onto the flat tire, and I explained my dilemma.

"Jump in. I'll take you back to a station where you can get that fixed."

Jimmy was returning from a selling trip in Tucson, and he had seen Armand. He had sold Pueblo pottery and jewelry to Dad for years and we all knew him.

He said Armand had told him about Red Lake, and he expressed his regrets. I told him I was headed to borrow some money from Armand, and I confessed that I didn't have any money for the repair. So after arriving at the gas station, Jimmy offered to share his cash. He pulled out his wallet—he had $15. He gave me $7 and said he would wait for me.

While the tire was being repaired, I went to the restroom and scrubbed the grit from my hands, and splashed my face with cool water. I bought a Coke and two candy bars, and paid $1.50 for the tire repair.

Jimmy drove me back to the propped-up Lincoln, and when the tire was on and he was sure all was well, he headed out of town again. I shook his hand heartily and thanked him profusely.

"When I get back in business, I'll be buying from you, Jimmy," I promised, trying hard to believe in the possibility.

But I came to find out that Tucson wouldn't offer me any windfall, either. Things had turned sour for Armand. All he could give me was $20 to get back home. But I didn't have a home. I didn't know where to go. No place to stay. Nothing to do. I felt even more shy. But I didn't want to show any weakness. Who do you show your feelings to? Who do you talk to? The only one I could talk to would be my wife, and she didn't want any part of me, because I was broke and busted and couldn't even buy a quart of milk for my kids. She didn't want me anywhere around any of them.

I stayed with Carl for a while in Lupton. He had rented a little house there, and he helped me get a job laying pipe with him. Soon after that Carl joined the Army.

I kept to myself.

I stopped in the store. I knew my parents couldn't help me. I had to help myself. Denny and Dewey were old enough to pump gas and work in the trading post now. And now Maxie and Mildred were back in Lupton. Maxie and Sonny McCarrell, Esther's husband, worked the store. Esther was down the highway at home with a bunch of kids. The trading post couldn't support any more families.

Aggie and his wife, Rosemary, were there struggling with a growing family, too. Aggie had even moved an abandoned railroader's house that sat next to the tracks — moved it closer to the store — so they would have a place to live.

I grabbed a Coke and a candy bar and wandered outside. I didn't want to tell anyone what was really happening.

James Goodluck strolled toward me from across the highway, the traditional Navajo scarf that wrapped his forehead and tied at the back of his head was crooked as usual.

"I'm sure happy to see you, Gilbert," he said, with his clipped Navajo accent.

"Happy to see you, too, James," I muttered, trying to be polite.

James ambled into the store with greetings for everyone, and soon the laughter spilled out to where I slumped against the building. Maybe I should join them. James Goodluck always brought laughter with him. But not for me. Not today.

I pulled the wallet from the back pocket of my jeans, opened it and stared. I had expected it to be bulging with bills by now. The wallet held a couple of dollars and the crinkly poem.

Taking the poem out, I unfolded it and slid down against the building to read it. Over and over I read it — especially the last stanza.

> *Success is failure turned inside out—*
> *The silver tint of the clouds of doubt.*
> *And you never can tell how close you are,*
> *It may be near when it seems afar;*
> *So stick to the fight when you're hardest hit,—*
> *It's when things seem worst that you must not quit.*

I closed my eyes and concentrated on that final stanza. My mind drifted to my dreams of success — now tainted and scarred. But a dream is a dream. Was it so bad to still have the dream, the passion to succeed? How could I possibly go after it again? I had no other choice. Well, it couldn't get any worse, I thought, so the hell with it. Give it another try. I was busted, broke, humiliated. All those things that people fear, that dangle in front of them to keep them from taking chances, had already happened to me. I chose to see that as the cure. Besides, dreams aren't born of money. I still had hope. Empty pockets full of hope.

When I opened my eyes, I stared into the same picture I had seen since childhood. The rugged landscape endured, with its beauty and strength. Now, I had to endure. I had to persist.

Then I walked into the store and looked around. I knew my dad had worked hard, but he didn't really want what I wanted. I would be frustrated staying here and would want to change things and not be able to try it. It made me nervous and anxious to see the potential to do more business. But Dad had always said, "Be careful, be careful." He was careful, maybe I wasn't. But, I had to be in business. It was my destiny. I had to be willing to take chances, make mistakes, be aggressive, competitive and savvy. I told myself I couldn't worry about what people thought. I had to do it my way—have the determination to succeed.

I loved to work. I could work longer and harder than anyone. I deserved to be successful. Why would I work that hard for anyone but myself? If I had myself as an employee, I could make myself rich. And that's what I'm going to be, the best employee I ever had.

But, there were no short cuts. In the meantime I had to make some money, so I job-hopped for a while.

I hung out at Dad's store and felt alone. Sometimes Linda would let Gayle come and stay in Lupton for a few days. She was about 5 then.

Eventually, Linda and I got back together again. We moved to Scottsdale, and I worked for Bill McGee in Old Town. We found a little apartment. Linda got a job at Motorola, and Grace came to help with the kids.

McGee's Indian Den sat on the south side of First Avenue, about a block east of the Sugar Bowl ice cream parlor. I worked hard and paid attention to every detail of the business, and I learned more.

Then Armand called and said he had leased the Hopi House on Route 66 near Winslow. He asked me to open it and run it for him while he finalized everything so he could leave Tucson. We had to try something.

Of course, I agreed, even knowing how broke we both were. We had to keep trying. We didn't have money for merchandise, but I told him we would figure something out.

Creative Financing

"I paced the floor, desperate for a way to get money."

The Hopi House sat west of Winslow on an open plain of high barren desert where so much gritty wind had blown across the land that the rocks had lost their jagged edges — the smooth stones that covered the dirt had literally been tumbled by nature.

The April wind pounded the landscape with a vengeance the day we arrived, but it couldn't sweep away my determination. The store, a typical highway store, stretched along Route 66 and had two gas pumps out front, covered by a large awning.

And there was plenty of room for the family. Highway homemaking took on new hope for Linda with the two-story living quarters attached to the store. The living room and kitchen were downstairs, and two bedrooms upstairs. The four kids shared one huge bedroom. Even Grace came to pitch in with the kids who ranged from about three to seven years old. Linda was only about 23 herself.

I hired Johnny Baquersa, a Hopi guy from Winslow, to help set up the store and the snack bar. I went to one of the traders we knew and got some jewelry on credit, and one of our old souvenir suppliers gave us merchandise on credit, too. We could get a small start that way.

But I had to find a way to buy a load of gasoline — and lumber and paint for signs — so we could start taking in some money.

I paced the floor, desperate for a way to get money. I couldn't go to the bank. My credit stunk. Then I got an idea — I had a plan. I explained it to Johnny, and he agreed.

I told Johnny to go to Pacific Finance in Winslow and apply for a loan for $500 supposedly to buy furniture for his house — which, if approved, he would lend to Armand and me. We promised to pay the loan back, and give Johnny $50 cash for making the deal. Johnny told the loan officer that he was working for Gilbert and Armand Ortega at the Hopi House. The lender knew us and gave me a call — just like I predicted.

"Mr. Ortega, your employee Johnny Baquersa is here requesting a loan, and he needs a cosigner," the lender hesitated. "Would you be willing to cosign for him?"

"Well, normally I wouldn't," I paused as if considering the proposition.

"But Johnny is a really good worker, very dependable, so just this once I'll sign for him."

I hung up the phone and breathed a huge sigh of relief, then raced to the finance office and cosigned the note. Then I waited, *"Standing on a Corner in Winslow, Arizona,"* waiting for Johnny to get the $500. When we met, Johnny handed me the cash. After giving Johnny his $50, we went to the station and paid $300 for a load of gasoline to be delivered, then bought the plywood, two-by-fours, and the paint that we needed for signs with the $150 that was left. It took us over two weeks to paint and build the signs. We put them up along the highway advertising gasoline, snacks, souvenirs, and encouraging people to turn off to Hopi House.

A few days later, all the signs on the north side of the highway, attracting traffic traveling west, had been chopped down by the rancher who owned the property. I tried everything to convince him to let us put the signs back up — shade for the cows, you name it. But he refused. So we only had signs on the south side of the highway for the traffic returning from the west along Route 66.

Hopi House showed promise. Linda helped in the store and the snack bar. The kids ran in and out of the store, but always knew how to act with customers. They were polite and respectful.

One day, from the upstairs bedroom, the kids spotted a skunk lurking around the garbage cans behind the store.

"Dad, Dad," Gayle Dean screamed.

"That skunk just jumped into the garbage can."

All we needed was a skunk. I ran out and slammed the lid on and as fast as I could, and put the metal can in the back of the pickup. The kids watched from upstairs as I sped off to the dump, turned the can over, opened it. As the skunk ran, so did I and dove into the cab of the truck and zoomed off back to the store. A skunk wouldn't have been a good roadside attraction.

But we did have a bird.

In those days, we felt we needed a draw and this time it was "Hopi Joe," a Mynah bird. He was the store's mascot, and he greeted all the female customers with a wolf whistle. It was fun to watch them glance toward the source of the whistle — somewhat annoyed, somewhat flattered — then see the bird. His name was on the cage, so tourists would stroll by and say "Hi, Hoppy Joe" — the bird promptly corrected them,"Hopi Joe, Hopi Joe."

We always tried to come up with ideas to stop more traffic — hire Indian dancers, bring in snow, you name it. We had a constant stream of ideas, but never did any of those things. And one of our problems was that the only signs we could use were for traffic coming from the west, because that rancher had torn the others down. The better traffic flows from the east, where you have more states to draw from. But, of course, those vacationers have to come back, too.

Naturally, we still needed cash, so when Armand got there with the remainder of his Tucson inventory, we took some jewelry with a retail value of about $10,000 into Holbrook and pawned it for $1,500. We could never get that jewelry back. We needed the cash flow so badly, we never had an extra $1,500 to pull out.

When Armand, Marie and their family arrived, we had to rent a little house in Winslow. Linda got a job, and Grace took care of the kids. Gayle and Desireé went to the new Bonnie Brennan Elementary School in Winslow, along with Armand and Marie's younger kids. Their older kids went to the high school. Armand, Jr. was on the track team and would run along Route 66 from the Hopi House to Winslow and back for practice.

In spite of all of our struggles, we had fun at Hopi House, and we began doing business, too. Our families were together, and we were starting over.

And we laughed a lot, and played practical jokes on one another.

One I remember vividly. It was more of a practical "choke." Everyone knew I loved strawberry soda pop, and I could toss down a bottle in seconds. So one day, Linda and Armand, Jr. put *Tabasco* in my pop. I chugged it down as usual. Well, they were over by the showcases snickering — until they saw me. It took my breath away, and I started choking and sputtering. When I couldn't breathe, they got scared. With watery eyes and raspy throat, I revived.

It's a good thing Armand, Jr. could run fast.

Gilbert helped Armand open the Hopi House, west of Winslow, in the mid-1960s.

Gayle Dean, Desirée, Renée and Gilbert, Jr. at home in Winslow
The girls are wearing squaw dresses made by their Aunt Esther.

This Exit, Gilbert Ortega

"The road to success is always under construction."

The highway was changing and great lengths of Interstate 40 were beginning to appear. The rest was still in the planning stage. Route 66 would eventually disappear as the main street of the southwest, replaced by the interstate highway with exits at interchanges. A new era was beginning. and I wanted to be part of it. Besides, Hopi House was running smoothly, and it was time for me to strike out on my own again. I probably had all of $1,500. And I was already 29 or 30 years old. I couldn't wait any longer.

I took Linda and the kids back to Lupton, where I leased some reservation land from a Navajo resident, John Tin Smith, at an interchange where Interstate 40 was coming through. It was about 500 yards from Dad's store. Red Lake had left me with one asset, my Indian Trader's license. I needed it to go into business at this reservation location. And it felt good to be back in Lupton. I had come full circle. Now I needed to make something happen.

We rented a tiny three-room block house. It was painted pink and had a turquoise door and sat on a dusty spot within walking distance to Dad's store. We squeezed in and settled into our new home. But, we had to make the living room into a bedroom. Nothing much had changed in Lupton — except for all the pickup trucks everybody drove. Linda did a good job of "highway homemaking," and the kids went to school in Sanders.

While Lupton felt comfortable, familiar and safe, the new super highway coming through spelled "opportunity." All my instincts and senses were tuned to the possibilities which that interchange held for me. I got to work immediately.

With the $1,500 I had saved from the Hopi House, I bought cinder block and some 3rd-grade lumber from the sawmill at Navajo. I envisioned the store in my head and traced the rectangular outline into the dirt with a large stick, so the entrance would face the traffic exiting the highway. I needed a work crew. My brother Denny was in college at ASU, but Carl Kempton, my brother Dewey, and Freddie Slatten were all there to help so we could begin construction. Carl had just returned from three years in the Army with even more skills — and he was an eager worker.

At a glance, Carl inventoried the building supplies, then shook his head in disapproval.

"Gilbert, we don't have enough block," he huffed, pointing to the stacks of block.

"What do you mean, Carl?"

"Well, look. There's no way we can build the store with this. We need more materials."

"I don't have money for more block, Carl."

I shoved my hands in my jean pockets and stomped across the store layout on the ground, looked at the block, looked at the perimeter of the would-be store. I paced in silence for several minutes. The others just stood there. It was imperative that this store be built with what we had. And we couldn't afford to waste any time either. There was no way to create more money or more cinder block. Suddenly I had it, and snapped my fingers.

"We just have to cut corners. We'll build a triangular store."

Well, they just stared at me like I was crazy, like I was a regular "Frank Lloyd Wrong."

"Stores don't have to have four sides. Hogans have eight."

I snatched the stick and literally cut corners in the earthen diagram. The widest portion still faced the interchange.

I figured if we built wooden teepees at each corner, it would look like it was intentional — not like a triangular trading post, but an Indian Village. And that's what I called it, Indian Village. The Fawlettes built a Chevron station at the same time, so that solved the need for gasoline.

The building went up in no time — cutting corners helped to speed up construction. Many of our Navajo neighbors who saw us at work offered to pitch in. "Oh, I'll help you, Gilbert," each would say. We were all the best of friends and they would help us with anything.

Even James Goodluck, showed up with one of his philosophical comments. "The road to success is always under construction," he chimed. Boy, was he right.

Maxie built a restaurant next to the store — customers entered through the teepee at the back corner. That filled another need, another attraction. Later, we had family parties and dances there sometimes.

I hired Albert Lewis, a local Navajo artist, to paint colorful figures and designs on the store and on the wooden teepees, too. So, Indian

Village was brightly painted, and the teepees at each corner were very effective.

We also built the teepees out of that 3rd-grade lumber. Since the cheap wood had big knot holes, we hammered pieces of tin cans into the gaps, and Albert managed to paint over our patches just fine.

Next I had him make the highway signs. They were extremely important. For the EXIT sign, he insisted on using a ruler and making the lines straight. He wouldn't do it freehand. I paid him $6 a sign.

I always tried to save money. I kept track of sign supplies and would make Albert and the others check in their hammers at the end of the day — even fine someone $5 if they lost a hammer.

Albert finally got disgusted with the procedure.

"Gilbert, you treat me like *communism,*" he chided, handing me a beat-up hammer and a handful of nails at the end of the day.

Then we had to build displays, shelves, showcases. Uncle Earnest and I built the showcases, and Dad bought me the glass for the tops — at about $10 each. I lined the inside base of the showcases with deep burgundy velvet from Dad's store — the jewelry would look attractive placed on it. The store was taking shape. I got some Indian jewelry on credit, some on consignment, a few Navajo rugs, sandpaintings, pottery. I ordered lots of souvenirs, post cards, Mexican velvet paintings and leather goods.

Indian Village was colorful and unique. It got noticed, and people started pulling off the highway in droves — probably out of curiosity. And that was the start of something new for me. The traffic was turning.

Armand came by to visit and walked through the store, inspecting.

"Well, this will make a nice house if you don't do any business," he chuckled.

He was on the move again, too. I-40 was scheduled to bypass Hopi House, but it had been a money maker, so Armand purchased some property just east of Sanders at Cedar Point exit on the new highway — a stretch of acreage on a mesa on the north side of the highway. A perfect location for a store.

So we had both come full circle, and, boy, had we learned a lot.

In retrospect, I probably shouldn't have built a triangular store, because it came out smaller — I lost square footage. But by adding the teepees on the corners, I was able to make it look bigger from the highway. That angle really helped me. You could see that entire elongated side from the interstate.

We still needed signs, and built them out of the remaining 3rd-grade lumber, cutting more pieces of tin cans to cover the holes so the signs would look attractive from the highway. I offered several Navajos $50 a year to put up signs on their property. Signs like **"See Sandpaintings made by Indians at Indian Village."** They always accepted the agreement.

Customers never really asked if someone was there making sandpaintings on the premises, but the sign created that image. Besides permanent sandpaintings were a new phenomenon. By using permissable images or altering them in such a way that the sacred quality was not infringed upon, permanent sandpaintings became attractive handmade merchandise.

When we were first putting the signs up, I had a contest. Carl against Dewey and Freddie. Whoever could put the most signs up in a day would get $20. Dewey and Freddie put up four, Carl built three, so Dewey and Freddie got the $20. The next morning, the first gust of wind that blew knocked Dewey and Freddie's four signs down. Carl's stayed up. I tried to get the bonus back from Dewey, but he said he already spent it. So I made them put the signs back up.

Dewey was a force waiting to happen. He was handsome and talented, and anxious for his turn to prove himself. I saw a lot of myself in Dewey and knew his trials and tribulations would someday pay off. He and Freddie Slatten were great friends.

Now, I needed one more sign — a large one for the store's rooftop. We built a big 30' x 12' "Indian Village" sign, advertising the store and restaurant. We anchored it to the rooftop support beam of the store and held it down with huge cables that were tied to each side of the sign and stretched down from the rooftop sign and attached to metal stakes pounded into the ground.

This was against every sign code known to man.

But we just did it. Every time the wind blew — which was constantly — the sign creaked, and Carl and I would race outside and hold onto the cables and keep the sign from blowing off the roof. It could have killed someone.

Another problem was the flooring in the store. It was that cheap lumber, too, and people kept getting the heels of their shoes caught in the holes. Freddie Slatten used the gaps as targets for pitching nickels and quarters. He could put them right through the cracks.

But the billboards were working, and the triangular trading post was attracting business. Cars were stopping, merchandise was flying out, and I began building my inventory. And I put up more signs, better signs. They were the advertisement of the highway — they had to lure, entice. I continued to offer an annual fee to Navajo property owners along the highway for sign placement. They continued to accept my agreement.

Lupton became a hub of Ortega ingenuity, and Dad even changed the name of his store to "Max Ortega and Sons Trading Post." By 1967, it was like a compound with all our families there. Kids rode bikes and played together. I had coffee with Mom every morning. She was the first to get a TV in Lupton, and we would gather at Mom and Dad's on Sunday evenings to watch Ed Sullivan.

Salesmen would come and go and stop for coffee and visit. Bernarr De Priest showed up in his old station wagon, packed with merchandise, and I bought a barrel of Jemez pottery from him. The small thick clay pots were handpainted with traditional Indian designs using poster paints in bright and even fluorescent colors — a crude contrast to the beautiful pottery that has evolved. He also sold some of Leroy's jewelry. It was clean and well made. I could only buy a little, though.

Eventually, Jimmy Silva appeared, and I was happy to see him. I bought some pottery from him. I had paid him back the $7.00 when I was at the Hopi House, but I took him to lunch at Maxie's Village Kitchen, and we laughed, reminiscing about the flat tire incident outside of Tucson.

I finally felt a glimmer of hope with Indian Village, like God had put his hand on me. That store felt like my greatest accomplishment, and I put all my energy into the business. I didn't have any competition. I was the first one on I-40. The signs led the customers to me: **Exit Now, Turn Here.**

Even though Linda, the kids and I were squeezed into that little three-room house, there was always room for nieces and nephews — we had wall-to-wall kids. I made sure Linda always prepared extra food in case anyone stopped by. In the evenings, I liked to tell the kids scary stories, stories about *skinwalkers* and other Navajo superstitions. There in our remote corner of the reservation, the windy blackness outside made my stories come alive for them as they huddled together, hanging on my every word.

And the kids loved comic books — especially Richie Rich. When I would read them Richie Rich comic books, I still pictured myself being rich someday. I could see it. I could feel it.

The store was doing enough business for us to get a bigger place, so we rented a red and white house about ten miles east in Manuelito, near the cliff dwellings. I was absorbed in the store and worked constantly. Things seemed to be turning around for me, though. Even Linda's mother saw some hope — she actually put a down payment on a house for us in Gallup. That gave Linda and the kids more stability, living in a real town. Gayle was almost 10 by then and would be starting fifth grade — the rest of the kids were right behind.

A photo taken several years later shows the now dilapidated tiny house where Gilbert, Linda and children lived in Lupton.

Ortega children arrive in Lupton, 1966
From left: Gilbert Jr., Gayle Dean, Desirée, Renée.

Several different views of Indian Village, Gilbert's first venture in Lupton, 1966.

Postcard of Gilbert's Indian Village and Max, Jr.'s restaurant in Lupton, 1966.

The Bitter Winds of Change

Mom and Dad were always encouraging. I still had coffee with Mom every morning and she was always anxious to hear about my business. One morning, she wasn't feeling well. She told Dad she was nauseous, had a pain running up her left arm, and was having a hard time breathing. Dad rushed her to the hospital in Gallup. I followed in my car.

She had a heart attack. In those days, there wasn't much doctors could do, so they sent her home to rest and recuperate. I was stunned. It seemed to have slowed her a bit; even though she was only about 51 then.

Armand and I felt so bad. We wanted her to be comfortable and enjoy life. So, we went to Phoenix and financed a new doublewide trailer to be delivered and set up there behind the store. She was thrilled with her trailer. She had never had a new home and this was the best we could do. Armand and I were committed to making the payments — whatever it would take. The thought that my mother's health was vulnerable shook me to the core. She had given me so much strength and I wanted to do the same for her. I visited her daily and she appeared fine and healthy, and she and Dad enjoyed the comfort of their new home.

Gilbert's parents, Max, Sr. and Amelia in 1967 in their new trailer in Lupton.

Christmas in Lupton, 1967, Gilbert, Jr., Max, Sr., Gilbert.

Ortega children with Grandma Grace in front of her trailer at cliff dwellings near Manuelito, New Mexico.

Hopes and Aspirations

*"I was scratching at the door of success, but I wanted in. I could see it.
I could feel it. I could hear it calling me."*

Something sparked in me, igniting new desire toward accomplishment. Indian Village had given me a window of hope, and I realized that one store wasn't enough. I wasn't satisfied. I could handle more. I wanted to do more business. I was scratching at the door of success, but I wanted in. I could see it. I could feel it. I could hear it calling me.

Sometimes, I wondered where my business sense came from — the desire that burned in me to achieve more. Maybe it was from my great grand-father. I don't know. I just knew I didn't want to stop. My dad took good care of his business, but he didn't want to grow. There's nothing wrong with that. He just wasn't the type to want more. At one time, he was offered almost every store on Route 66 for practically nothing. Armand and I would have jumped at an opportunity like that. We would have taken those stores and quadrupled the business.

Actually, Dad did better than anybody on the highway and supported seven children with that store. When I-40 spread across the scene, he was bypassed, too. But most of his business was with the Navajos, so that didn't change.

By then, Maxie had found a location in Joseph City, west of Holbrook. He opened Sitting Bull Indian Store there. Aggie had set up Navajo sandpainting production in Lupton, and I bought sandpaintings from him for my store. Later he would open a retail trading post of his own. Armand's Indian Ruins store at Sanders was doing extremely well.

The cash flow became stable and consistent. I was able to build up my inventory and do more business. Overhead expense on the highway was minimal, which allowed room for profit. And finally, I began to conquer the debts from Red Lake. Though it took a few years, eventually I paid back most of the people — some forgave the debts — some settled for 50 cents on the dollar.

And I couldn't have done it without people like Carl Kempton. He's a great guy, and the best student I ever had — very intelligent. He would listen and learn, and could think just like me. Talking to Carl was like talking to myself. Freddie Slatten was also a hard worker. Carl and Freddie both became very successful. Actually, Lupton produced quite a few millionaires, for an unassuming, sparsely populated reservation town.

Shortly thereafter, I was approached to buy a store called Geronimo just west of Holbrook. The store was small and old, and there was a tiny house next to it. I made a deal for the land and the store, but I hadn't done anything with it yet. Then, I saw it as an opportunity for Carl. He was ready. And it was a way I could pay his parents back for lending me $3,500 for Red Lake, for believing in me.

I told Carl I would help him select the merchandise, get him credit with the vendors, and charge him $300 a month rent. He would have a store and a house. I would work with him for a year, then start charging him $1,000 a month. Carl snapped up the chance and never stopped. He knew how to work. He took off like a whirlwind. He was willing to work seven days a week, from sun-up to sundown. Then I sold him the property. Later, he built a beautiful new store with elegant living quarters. He had that extra push. Once he built that new store, his business quadrupled. Carl and I went through a lot together, and I was very proud of him.

Finally, we were all seeing some success.

The Grievous Winds of Sorrow

My youngest brother Dewey and his fiancée Susan were living in Lupton and expecting a baby. Dewey still liked to go into Gallup once in a while to visit frriends and have some fun. This time, it was nearly morning, August 25, 1968, when he headed home to Lupton. He must have fallen asleep at the wheel, and he swerved off the highway and rolled his Volkswagen — there at the state line, minutes from home. He was thrown out of the car onto a muddy patch along the highway. He died there — across from the truck stop. Because his body lay on the state line of Arizona and New Mexico, it created confusion about legal jurisdiction, and they couldn't move him until it was resolved. It was horrific. Mom and Dad were in shock. They called me and I rushed from Gallup. Linda drove me to Lupton because I was too shaken to drive. When we got there, he was still laying there in the mud on the side of the highway, dead.

When I saw him, it felt like someone punched me in the chest. I couldn't move. I was gasping and shivering. Mom was sobbing. Dad stood there helpless, pale and distant. I didn't know what to do.

Dewey's death was overwhelming for Mom and Dad. They had lost their youngest son. Handsome and lively, and full of expectations. Dewey was gone. My parents sank into despair. They were powerless in the face of death. It was unchangeable, unstoppable, like the constant wind that slammed against the vast landscape. They would never be the same.

From that day on, every time I drive by that spot along the highway, that picture of Dewey laying there dead flashes at me. It is seared in my memory. Dewey never had the opportunity to excel. He would have been a great success.

The Hollow Winds of Loss

Then Mom died.

I was heartbroken and shattered.

Dewey's death had been too much for her: it had only been three months since his accident. She said she wished she had just died a year earlier when she had her first heart attack.

"I can't live through another holiday without my baby," she cried.

Mom died November 27, 1968 — the day before Thanksgiving.

She had been sitting in the trailer visiting with her sister from Santa Fe, my Aunt Josie, when she complained of feeling ill — chest pain, shortness of breath. Dad was terrified because of her previous heart attack and he raced her to the hospital in Gallup. We all followed. Dad got her there, but she died in the hospital.

She was only 52. She could have started to enjoy herself.

Dad was devastated. The entire family was devastated.

My poor mother. We lost her entirely too soon. I never had a chance to prove how much her encouragement helped me to succeed. I wanted her to see my achievements.

But her love and inspiration continued to motivate me.

I still miss her.

Ingenuity

"Well, if you don't do any business here, Gilbert, this will make a nice house."

I took the poem my mother had given me and read it over and over again. At least it wasn't the only thing in my wallet anymore.

And I decided, it was high time for me to excel. First I had to replace that wedge of a store — make it bigger, better. I wasn't sure just how yet.

Then, on a trip to Showlow, I noticed a unique dome-style building that had been erected since my last visit. It caught my attention and fed my curiosity. I could use a building like that for a store, I thought, so I stopped and asked the owners about it. They told me that they bought the dome from a fellow in Black Canyon City.

This had possibility written all over it, and I headed to Black Canyon City a few days later. I met with Bill Woods, who built the geodesic domes and discussed building one on the reservation. The 3,000 square foot prefabricated domes were built of triangle-shaped sections of interlocking plywood and then coated with plastic. For $12,000, I could get a complete building, including wiring. Why not go from triangular to circular? This would work. And I did it. I replaced the triangular store with a dome — it was the fastest, most efficient way I could create an attractive, noticeable store in the least amount of time. I could never have done it for less time or less money any other way.

After the dome was constructed, Albert Lewis went to work again with his paintbrush. He decorated it with Indian hoop dancers and sun face kachinas. We topped it off with a sign: **Gilbert Ortega's Indian Village**. I wanted my name on it. The store stood out like a giant decorated igloo against the rugged landscape. We made a makeshift teepee to cover the gas pumps using two-by-fours and roofing paper, so the cars could drive right in, gas up, then park in front of the store.

We built more showcases, displays, shelves. We jammed every inch of that store with merchandise: souvenirs, salt and pepper shakers, shot glasses, ash trays, headdresses, tomahawks, drums, moccasins, pottery, baskets, post cards, film. And, this time, more Indian jewelry. The showcases were full of jewelry. Rings, earrings, and bracelets sold the fastest. The walls displayed a few Navajo rugs, long sweeping headdresses, Mexican velvet paintings, even mounted bull horns. And more and more silversmiths, weavers, and other artisans came by to sell to me.

Just before the store opened, Armand stopped by. Always looking the businessman, he wore dress slacks, dress shirt and sport coat — and a beautiful Zuni bolo tie. He glanced around in predictable fashion, then strolled over to where I stood. I already knew what he was going to say.

"Well, if you don't do any business here, Gilbert, this will make a nice house."

But I did do business — lots of business.

Since Maxie had opened his store outside Joseph City, we had no cafe. I bought a little trailer — '50s diner style — and called it the Coffee Cup. It served its purpose, but didn't do much business. It had only 10 seats, and we served prepared and packaged snacks and homemade tuna sandwiches.

In the summer I would take Gayle and Desirée — and sometimes my niece Cindy, when she stayed with us — to work with me. I'd wake them about 5:30 a.m., and we would head from Gallup to Lupton to open for business. The kids would help in the store, and sometimes by the end of the day, they would hang out at the Coffee Cup. It was usually 8 p.m., by the time I locked up the store and drove back to Gallup — without them.

I was so absorbed in business, I completely forgot them. This didn't happen just once. Linda would call Dad and tell him to watch out for the kids until I got there. Then I would turn around and go 20 miles back to Lupton and pick them up — a 40-mile round trip mistake. But I did it again and again.

When we would leave in the morning, Linda would say, "Don't forget the kids today." Then she would turn and remind them, "You kids make sure that Dad doesn't forget you." Gilbert, Jr. and Renée were still too little to come along — or I would have forgotten them, too.

I guess I was preoccupied — determined to open another store. I started looking for the best location. There was a spot west of Houck, off an interchange that I liked, a highly visible mesa that looked down on the highway. It was on the north side of the I-40, but a store could easily be seen from a distance in either direction. This was reservation land, but I knew I could arrange a lease for a percentage of gross sales and use my Indian Trader's license.

It was about then that Joe Atkinson stopped by. He and his brother Lynn had struck out on their own, too. Joe was considering a reservation lease venture also, and he asked me to go to Window Rock with him. I left the store in good hands, and we backtracked a little, and I showed him the spot I wanted near Houck. It looked good to him too, and I intended to pursue it immediately. I planned to put another dome there — a bigger one.

Then Joe and I headed toward Window Rock. It was a crisp morning, bright and clear. The cottonwoods were budding and the piñons glistened. As we drove along, we watched sheep graze lazily. Ahead a dusty-colored horse munched on some wild grasses near the highway.

Joe took one hand off the steering wheel, snapped his fingers and pointed.

"Is that Sandy?" he quipped, laughing.

I rolled the window down, playing along.

"Sandy?" I called, then whistled.

Of course, the horse never lifted his head.

"Give it up, Joe. You've got to quit looking for that horse," I teased.

Soon we approached the russet-colored sandstone hill the town was named for — Window Rock — the huge natural gap that opened through the center of the 200 ft. buff of sandstone. The capital of the Navajo Nation since 1936, Window Rock was an important location for the tribe. Joe and I each submitted proposals for our new ventures.

A few months later, I opened Indian City on the leased reservation land west on I-40 at Houck. The dome was larger than Indian Village and had a mezzanine that I jammed with rugs, moccasins, and leather goods. On the main floor, six showcases formed a square in the center, filled with handmade Indian jewelry, trays of rings, racks of bracelets, layers of earrings, and more. Displays of much of the same merchandise that I sold at Indian Village filled the store. Every visible place was merchandised. Every inch of contoured wall held rugs, paintings, baskets.

The outside was brightly painted with hoop dancers and sun faces like Indian Village. Here I put in a full service Exxon station, and a colorful teepee sat out front. I even bought a better grade of lumber from the sawmill for signs, so we didn't have to cover the knot holes with tin cans this time. We hauled such a heavy pickup load of lumber that when we hit a bump in the road, the front tires would bounce off the pavement. And better billboards led the way to ***Gilbert Ortega's* Indian City.**

The store started doing business immediately — and even more business than Indian Village was doing. The location was great — and, besides, I had learned more and it showed in the store, in the merchandise, the jewelry, the displays. And I really promoted Indian jewelry.

Though the timing wasn't good, Bernie VanderWagen, Linda's dad, offered me the chance to buy his ranch south of Gallup. It was 3,000 acres on the road to Zuni. It spread out on both sides of the highway in an area that was appropriately named VanderWagen, New Mexico. Heavily wooded with piñon, the portion east of the highway had a lovely ranch house nestled into a quiet slope. Bernie wanted $150,000. He would take $10,000 down and $1400 per month. This was an enormous amount of money, but an irresistible opportunity. Besides, I knew I could sell 50 acres that would pay for the whole thing — and I did.

Buying the ranch was a decision I never regretted.

I did regret not spending enough time with my family, though. I worked constantly. The business invigorated me. It was more like a hobby. I loved it.

I tried to spend more time with my family. I took Linda and the kids to the ranch for a few days here and there. I even took everyone to Disneyland.

Then I decided to coach Desireé's basketball team. She was 12 by then. Well, I worked those girls into shape. They practiced and practiced — and complained about too much practicing. I wouldn't let them quit. And soon they went from whining to winning. When they won the championship, they understood the value of hard work and perseverance. They were proud of themselves.

Linda and I went out more — we actually had a social life for a while. That seemed to please her. Maybe she had started to believe in me again. I hoped so.

But, ultimately, it didn't last. Business would always come first.

A few years later, she finally had had it with me. She had her reasons. And we were fighting a lot. I knew the end was near when I walked into the house, opened the refrigerator, then scooped a spoonful of jello right out of the middle of the mold she had chilling for dinner — and she threw me out. I had to go and live at the ranch.

*Brothers, Max, Jr. and Gilbert at the new
Indian Village in Lupton.*

Gilbert with artist, Charles Damrow.

The family at their new home in Gallup, 1969. From left, Gayle Dean, Desireé, Reneé, Linda, Gilbert, Gilbert, Jr.

Bernie VanderWagen, Linda's father and Gilbert, 1968.

Gilbert and Linda in Jamaica in 1970 – their very first vacation.

*Gilbert put another dome at
Houck, Arizona along I-40.*

Indian City postcard.

*Every inch of Indian City was filled with merchandise — from velvet paintings,
Mexican leather, moccasins, souvenirs, and Indian jewelry.*

Red Rock Rockettes: 1971
New Mexico state champion girls' basketball team.
Bottom row from left to right: Lisa Schuelke, Rhonda
Sparks, Desirée Ortega, Valerie Estrada, Lydia Garcia.
Top row from left to right: Deava Cato, Loretta
Bischoff,
Terri Rollie, Mary DeGiacoma, Laurie Christenson,
Gilbert Ortega, coach.

Transition Time

"My dad had taught me to be a good judge of people, and I developed this skill as I developed my businesses."

I was busy packing my two stores with curios, more and more Indian jewelry, rugs, baskets, pottery. I had been buying an assortment of Mexican leather goods from Bernardo Bawn, a Jewish immigrant from Juarez. When Bernardo sold his business in 1969, his assistant, Joaquin Torres, a native of Juarez, went on his own. And one day — on his first trip to the US — he showed up in Lupton with new leather merchandise. Joaquin was probably in his early twenties, well-groomed, and well-dressed. Later, as I got to know him better, I became impressed with his demeanor, his work ethic, and his intelligence.

Since it was his first selling time in the area, he wasn't sure what to expect and felt it was important to call on me personally. He looked surprised when he asked for Gilbert Ortega, and I stepped up to shake his hand. He told me later he expected someone older — I was just over 30. He said he pictured Lupton as an average town, but was amazed at how small it was — only four or five stores and a truck stop, a few tiny houses, and the dome. He had never seen anything like that dome before. And he had never seen Navajos or hogans either.

I sent Joaquin thirty miles west on I-40 to service my Indian City store. This dome was a little larger and had an Exxon gas station. I encouraged him to call on Armand, Maxie, Aggie, Carl Kempton, and Joe Atkinson, too, thinking he might make some more sales. He was appreciative of the business. I liked Joaquin. My dad had taught me to be a good judge of people, and I developed this skill as I developed my businesses. I invited Joaquin to come to work for me anytime he wanted to move from Mexico.

Somehow, I knew that if I wanted to be at the core of this business, I needed to be in Gallup where I could buy and sell jewelry — and break through into a wholesale operation, adding another facet to the business possibilities. Then, in 1970, I found a location in the heart of downtown Gallup at 120 W. Coal, a block north of Route 66. The store front offered two huge display windows and inside showcases lined the perimeter of the store. Tex Giger had worked day and night, building those showcases and fixtures. Nellie Etsitty, his wife, worked in the store and has continued working with me for 30 years now. It has been hard-working, honest people like them who have helped to make me who I am.

Gallup was the hub for Indian arts and crafts commerce. I began buying in larger quantities from Navajo and Zuni silversmiths. Silversmiths would line up with crinkled brown lunch sacks full of handmade rings, earrings and bracelets. I bought everything I could and filled the 3 x 6 vault. And I bought from Leroy Atkinson, as well. He was probably the best in the business. His silversmiths made beautiful jewelry. With Jimmy Long and his family, Leroy developed a unique design and style — clean, shiny Navajo silver jewelry, using lots of turquoise and coral.

Now I wanted to make a name for myself — a name *of* myself, I guess. No more "Many Goats," "Indian Village," or "Indian City" store names. I called the store **Gilbert Ortega**. In the lettering of the logo, I suggested the letter **"t"** in Ortega should look like a cross — for my mother, for her belief in me, and to honor her memory. It was like having my signature on the store, with her blessing.

In order to succeed, I also needed good people to work for me. It was the spring of 1973, when Joaquin decided to take my offer and called the store in Lupton. But I was in Gallup at the new store. A lot had happened since I had seen him, and his timing was excellent.

Joaquin obtained a work permit, and I sent him money for the trip. He now had a wife and infant son. Joaquin would become a great asset. When he arrived, we sat in my office on Coal Street, and I told him I wanted my business to grow and make money. I confided my failures and my problems to him and explained how I wanted to breakthrough into the wholesale business. I needed someone I could trust to work with me. He understood and made the commitment. He started as assistant manager at Lupton and Houck, and he dug his heels into the business and learned quickly.

Joaquin and his wife stayed with me at the ranch for a while. Since Linda and I were separated, she needed the house in town so the kids could go to school. I lived at the ranch, 16 miles south of Gallup. It wasn't long before I found Joaquin and his wife a doublewide trailer in Gallup, then took them to Showlow to buy a new car — the first new car they had ever owned. He, like many other early employees, is still with me today. And I appreciate the loyalty.

I needed good advisors, as well. When people see you work hard, a force takes over and help comes your way. I always asked for advice. It's amazing that when asking for advice, you become the recipient of a treasure trove of knowledge. You would be surprised at how people will help if you allow them to.

One example was the assistance I received from David Ruiz. A Gallup banker, he helped me financially and personally. He showed me what bankers look for — bottom line, net profits — liquid assets. If I hadn't asked his advice, I may not have gotten his help. By that time I had three stores, two with gas stations, and approximately 20 employees. If I wanted to advance, I would need the assistance of a banker.

GILBERT ORTEGA shows some of the new merchandise in his shop, Ortega's Indian Arts, at 120 W. Coal Ave. The shop, open seven days a week from 9 a.m. to 9 p.m. features a complete selection of Southwest Indian arts and crafts, especially handmade Navajo, Zuni and Hopi jewelry, as well as hand-painted Grecian items in copper, Gregorian hand-hammered copper, hand-painted porcelain, wood carvings, ceramics and candles.

*As appeared in the <u>Gallup Independent</u>
Early 1970s*

Turquoise Tornado

Indian jewelry was the style — the rage – it was in vogue.

I worked feverishly to build my wholesale business. My mind never stopped, always thinking of how to improve, expand, increase sales. Besides, Indian jewelry was beginning to experience a broader appeal and style.

It was definitely the style in Gallup. The locals, particularly those of us in the business, had our own style. The gals were "cowgirl-chic" in bell-bottomed jumpsuits with heavy silver and turquoise concho belts cinched around their hips, nugget necklaces, heishi or squash blossom necklaces, lots of bracelets and heavy earrings. And most topped off the look with bouffant hairdos. Many of the traders had a "business-western" look, and most wore heavy turquoise nugget watchbands, matching belt buckles, and bolo ties. Fancy cowboy boots in lizard or ostrich were a sign of success.

More people around the country started wearing Indian jewelry. Movie stars were seen in magazines sporting squash blossom necklaces and concho belts. Indian jewelry was gaining popularity on a grander scale, and I was in a position to profit from its popularity.

Then it hit. Like a turquoise tornado.

The Boom.

Indian jewelry was the style — the rage – it was in vogue. *The Wall Street Journal* called it an investment.

My business exploded — it was wildly successful. All the traders were experiencing the boom. Leroy Atkinson kicked into high gear, hiring more silversmiths. Joe Atkinson and his brother Lynn were in the middle of the boom, too. So was Armand. Gallup was the eye of the storm. Wholesale fed the whirlwind, and Indian jewelry stores lined the streets. Leroy told us to be careful. "When this ends, it will stop overnight like it did in WWII," he said.

Everyone wanted in the business. Buyers arrived from all parts of the country. Doctors wanted their wives to sell jewelry. Hippies, with cash stuffed in their boots, wanted to buy jewelry to sell to their friends. Even some gas stations put showcases inside and started selling Indian jewelry.

During the heyday, which lasted from about 1973 to 1976, I set the minimum wholesale purchase at $5,000. But I knew I couldn't just sit back and enjoy the windfall. I had to move fast — raise the bar. I devised a plan to start my own jewelry production and hire silversmiths. I got another location down the street at 201 W. Coal , with a large walk-in vault and a basement. It was a rich brown stucco building, painted with colorful rainbow dancers and sun gods. I designed a multi-stone inlay, a contemporary look — something new for the hungry market. Navajos do beautiful inlay work, different from the traditional Zuni style. I employed 20 Navajo silversmiths and set up production downstairs, fully equipped with the necessary tools and supplies. This meant that I had to spend a lot of time buying silver, turquoise, coral, various types of shell, and other supplies in large quantities. The silversmiths produced excellent quality and quantity. The main floor showcased the handmade contemporary line of Navajo inlay, and their work sold out quickly, over and over again. I wish I had a piece of that jewelry today.

It was then that I got an account with the Zales jewelry chain. They, like other jewelry retailers, would buy from us in Gallup on a regular basis. This increased our volume.

Everyone worked long hours. My kids helped, too. Gayle and Desirée were teenagers by then — old enough to learn the business. Gilbert, Jr. was in the basement buffing jewelry for the silversmiths when he was 12. Renée would help out too. Linda and I got along fine, even though we were divorced by then. We had no animosity between us, and still don't.

I worked harder than ever, but some evenings I would meet with other traders at The Talk of the Town, a club in the center of Gallup, or at Pal Joey's, another night spot. For me, they were meeting places with a purpose. It was a time to listen and learn, keep up with the pulse of the business, enjoy the bragging rights, check out the competition. I could get together with Joe Atkinson there, too, and I would tell everyone how Joe strutted around Lupton in his Roy Rogers gloves, boots, and badge when we were kids. They never knew whether to take me seriously or not. And he would go on about how I sold him the runaway horse, Sandy, when I was 12. But the conversations would always go back to all the traders' current successes.

I'm still in awe at whatever forces came together to create the Indian jewelry boom of the mid-seventies. One thing for sure, I was in the right place at the right time.

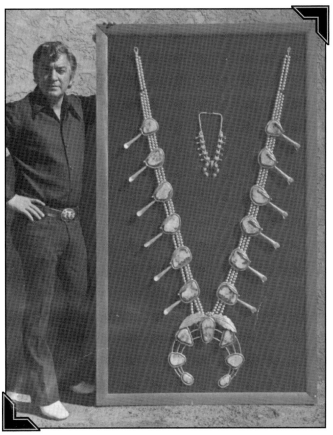

Gilbert standing by his "World's Largest Squash Blossom" Gallup, 1976.

*Jerry Apodaca, Governor of New Mexico from 1975-1979
and Gilbert.*

Brothers Gilbert and Armand
1974.

Armand and Leroy Atkinson, 1970s
Gallup.

Quicksilver

"It seemed like we were opening a store a month."

I never stopped. There was always someone to sell me something, show me something, offer me a deal. There were opportunities to do jewelry shows around the country. And there were more stores to open. It seemed like the bar was raising itself. I couldn't even take a deep breath. I worked 12 hours a day, seven days a week, and survived on about five hours of sleep.

That's when I bought a plane — a new eight-passsenger, twin-engine Cessna 402 — and hired a pilot. I was probably halfway on an ego trip when I bought that plane, but it helped me move even faster. Gallup airport had a landing strip where Frontier Airlines would land on its route to southern Colorado. The airport was dotted with small planes that traders had bought, since a lot of them were doing well. It was the new reservation status symbol, a giant step from the fancy cowboy boots. Armand had a plane. So did Joe Atkinson. A lot of us did jewelry shows and needed a way to transport ourselves and the merchandise. I did shows in Dallas, Houston, and Denver and took in tens of thousands of dollars. It became demanding and inconvenient selling like that, so in 1975, I created a catalog, *Gilbert Ortega Presents*. That was difficult too, since every item was different, and we couldn't always get the same things. However, it did help my name recognition in the Indian arts and crafts business and promoted my business across the country.

Then I started opening new stores. With Joaquin and my trusted crew, we opened a small store in Cubero, New Mexico, about 50 miles west of Albuquerque. An opportunity came about in Phoenix to start a retail/wholesale operation in a small location near 12th Street and Camelback. After we set it up, I sent Judy Yates there to run it. She had worked for me in Gallup and was a skilled manager. I could fly down there and check on things, then return to Gallup to finish the day's business. We were in the plane so much, that I thought I could fly it, too. I had taken some flying lessons years earlier, so I took over a few times, but Joaquin told me I flew the plane like a kid from Lupton in a hot rod, but that didn't make me want to stop trying.

I opened two stores in Dallas and sent my daughter Gayle and my Aunt Margie there to run them. No sooner was the last showcase merchandised than we flew back to Gallup and I bought the store at Continental Divide, 20 miles east of Gallup, from Lynn Atkinson, Joe's brother.

It seemed like we were opening a store a month. The crew had all worked nonstop for weeks on end without a day off, so I sent them all to Las Vegas to relax and have some fun.

By the time they got back, a new mall in Houston had contacted me, and I planned to open there, too. If I had to do it over again, you couldn't give me those stores in Dallas and Houston.

But soon a great opportunity presented itself. We met with a representative of the Chevron Corporation about the highway gas stations and discovered that a lease was coming available for the Fred Harvey complex at Cameron, the eastern entrance to the south rim of the Grand Canyon, north of Flagstaff along Highway 89.

Early the next morning, we flew to Cameron to study the possibilities. Cameron Trading Post was large and impressive, an historic complex built with thick stone walls, stone floors and heavy wooden beams. The operation included a large store, a restaurant facility, a motel, and of course, the Chevron station. It was an incredible tourist hub. Bus loads of tourists pulled in while we were there. The complex sat on a stretch of land that overlooked the Little Colorado. The store was huge, with plenty of retail space for Indian arts and crafts, gifts, souvenirs, and a small grocery store. One area sold bundles of wool yarn for rug weavers as well, as silver findings for jewelers, and other supplies for the Navajo artisans of the area. It was a business center in a remote area of the Navajo reservation.

Cameron became the biggest deal I made in the company's growth, the finest store I had ever owned, and the first to gross over $2 million. Cameron became my greatest accomplishment. During the transition to Cameron, a location came available at Coronado Mall, the busiest mall in Albuquerque, then two locations in Santa Fe, the Oldest House and the Oldest Church. And we opened those, also.

Now I needed headquarters. At the east end of Gallup along Route 66, I built a beautiful new red brick building with a showroom and a huge shop which accommodated 50 silversmiths. As part of the complex, I included a luxurious two-bedroom apartment upstairs. That way I could live with my true love — my business.

By that time, I was offered a location in the new Hyatt Regency being built in downtown Phoenix. I had ridden that turquoise tornado into 1977 and now owned 16 stores in Arizona, New Mexico and Texas. Even I was a little winded.

People said I was a workaholic, though I never felt like one because I loved what I did so much. It didn't feel like work, and I didn't — and don't — consider myself a workaholic. For example, take someone who loves gardening. If that person spends from morning until evening caring for the flowers, planting, weeding, would you call that individual a workaholic? My stores were as important to me as someone's garden or their home. That's where I spent my quality time.

Gilbert opened another store in Gallup during the jewelry boom of the mid-seventies and set up a silversmith operation.

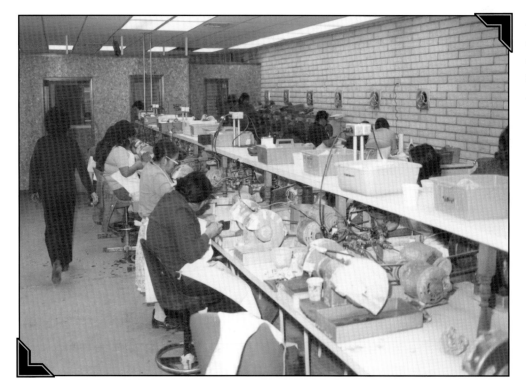

Navajo silversmiths hard at work in basement shop.

Gilbert, Jr. shown grinding a bracelet, learned the business as a youngster.

Continental Divide Trading Post on I-40 east of Gallup, NM.

An aerial view of the Cameron complex at east entrance to Grand Canyon, 1976.

A Gust of Sorrow

It was in May of 1977, that our family took another devastating blow. Aggie died of a heart attack. Rosemary had raced him from Lupton to the hospital in Gallup. I zoomed over to the hospital in a panic. The doctor confirmed that he had had a heart attack. I went in the room to see him. Armand got there from Sanders shortly after. Everyone who could, made it to the hospital as quickly as possible. We sat with him and reassured him that he would be just fine. He looked tired, so we left for a while. I went back to the store. It wasn't long after that I got the call that he had suffered another heart attack — and died.

Would we ever be without these tragedies chopping away at our family? Dad couldn't take much more. Poor Aggie. He had been doing so well at his store in Lupton and had just opened another outside Flagstaff. Rosemary and the kids were lost without him.

Turquoise Clouds and Silver Linings

"You have to be a fighter to stay on top, work harder."

It seemed like the wind was getting knocked out of everything — everything, including the turquoise tornado. By 1977, the Indian jewelry market was glutted. Some upstart businesses were wiped out. Long established traders geared down. I lost $600,000 to $700,000. But I had grown enough to withstand the setback. Adversity is like liquor. If you can't handle it, it will break you. You have to be a fighter to stay on top, work harder.

I began planning for the Hyatt Regency location in downtown Phoenix. I wasn't going to stop doing business because of a slump.

Heading into Pal Joey's one spring evening, I ran into Joe Atkinson, and he joined me. We met often for dinner, or coffee, or a drink, and we caught up on business. Joe had Atkinson's Trading Post, a large retail store, as well as a wholesale operation, and two smaller tourist locations in Gallup — Covered Wagon and Little Indian.

Joe said he had recently sold some real estate and was looking for a good investment, and said he might buy Cooper's Western chain.

"Buy my stores," I blurted out.

Joe had that same look on his face that he did when he was a kid and wanted to buy my horse. I knew my suggestion had sparked his interest.

So we did some figuring on a couple of cocktail napkins. We each signed the napkins, and I slipped mine into my shirt pocket when I left. That's how we always did business. A lot of very lucrative deals were made on napkins in Gallup.

The next morning, Joe went to his attorney and prepared an offer, and delivered it to my office a couple of days later, sliding it across the desk — his napkin attached. He offered $5 million for the chain. And I would keep my new building and wholesale business in Gallup and the Hyatt store planned for Phoenix. I knew the store he wanted the most was Cameron, and I didn't blame him for that. He was a smart businessman.

I signed the agreement, and we shook hands. The deal was made.

I had a two-year covenant not to compete, so I decided on something I had always wanted to do, and that was go to Nashville and record. Joe bet me $2,000 that I wouldn't do it, said I was just kidding.

But I was determined. I could still oversee my wholesale operation and pursue recording in Nashville.

Life-long friends, Joe Atkinson and Gilbert get together at Gilbert's art auction, March, 1995.

City
Home Delivery
Edition

THE TRUTH WELL TOLD

Independent

Only 24
Shopping Days
Until Christmas

NUMBER 265 VOLUME 90   GALLUP, NEW MEXICO 87301   WEDNESDAY, NOVEMBER 30, 1977

The King of Indian Jewelry Goes Country

By BONNIE MEYER, City Editor

GALLUP – Gilbert Ortega isn't sure how many of his 10,000 singles will sell, but one of his country western recordings will sell for $2,000.

"This is something I've wanted to do since I was 12," said the former "king of Indian jewelry." After Ortega sold all but two of his chain of Indian arts and crafts stores in three states, he decided to pursue his continuing interest and record country western music.

The $2,000 for the first record is a wager he won.

"One night I was sitting in Pal Joey's with Joe Atkinson (who bought the Ortega chain several months ago for $5 million) and I told him I was going to cut a record. He didn't believe me but said that he would give me $2,000 for the first record. I haven't given it to him yet, but here it is," said Ortega, holding up one of the single 45 rpms that he received Saturday.

The other 9,999 singles, featuring "Is It Wrong," and "Is This All There Is To a Honky Tonk" on the flip side, are being mailed out this week to disc jockeys at radio stations all over the country.

"Richie Johnson, who does national promotions out of Belen, is taking care of the mailings." Disc jockeys will receive the new single and a background information sheet on Ortega, along with a personal note.

"I started playing in high school and got my first guitar when I was 12," Ortega reminisced from his apartment above the one jewelry business he now operates.

"This is something I've always wanted to do." First, he contacted Johnson and sent him a tape. "That was back in May. He heard my tape and said it was time we went to Nashville."

In the country western capital of the world, Ortega arrived with 12 songs he was prepared to record. "It wasn't easy. We pared down a list of about 1,000 songs that we had worked on and translated."

One of Ortega's trademarks in his new venture will be bilingual songs. The words start out in English, then smoothly flow into Spanish.

"Ray Martinez of Gallup helped we. We worked for about three months on the transitions." Listening to the tape he brought back of the 12 songs that will be made into an album, the languages almost unnoticeable change.

Once in Nashville, Johnson hired a back up band, the Nashville Addition; Lloyd Green on the guitar; Pig Robbins on the piano; and Janie Fricke who does harmony.

The 15-piece back up musicians were carefully selected to blend with Ortega's voice and with the type of music he sings, he added.

"We spent 14 days there, practicing from 6 a.m. to 1 a.m. I selected 9 p.m. to 1 a.m. to cut the tapes. That was the best time for me when I felt I could best get with it."

Each of the 15 musicians and Ortega went into private sound booths, wearing the earphones that helped them hear all the other musicians.

"When the red light was on we were recording. When a white light was on we were practicing," Ortega explained.

Then, after the initial four hours of recording, came hundreds of more hours listening carefully to ... final ...

Gilbert Ortega

country western singers just dress naturally," he added.

Ortega said he isn't seeking public appearance during the record waiting period but this week he has been asked to appear in Dallas, Tex., at a farm conven... persons.

Al... ...

...hnson Buys Ortega Stores for $5 M...

...DONOVAN

... – Gilbert Ortega, ...naire, is no longer in ... business.
...ednesday that he had ...Joe Atkinson, also of ...Atkinson purchased ...s for $5 million ...s included 16 arts and ...read out through New ...ia, and Texas, and a ..., and supermarket in

...old Ortega owned two ...s in Gallup and land ...llup golf course. His com ...o, he had announced last

month, to build stores in San Diego or Los Angeles, in Honolulu and in the Hyatt House in Chicago.

Ortega began his career when he was 12 by selling a horse to the same Joe Atkinson for $50. He asked his father, who is now 75 and still active in the Indian trading business, what he should do with the money.

His father told him to "put it into jewelry and rugs." The young Ortega took his father's advice and soon turned the $50 into a $500 profit.

After graduating from Gallup High School, Ortega visited his brother, Armond, in Deming and looked over his brother's business, the Apache Village

Trading Post. He decided to go to work for this brother and learn the trading business firsthand.

By the time he was 21, he had made a small profit and had decided to go into big business. He thought there was an opportunity in the Navajo, N.M. area and decided to build a 7,000-square foot shopping center.

He leased the land from the Navajo Tribe and finally got the shopping complex built, only to see it go down in flames in a fire that destroyed the entire center. He had no insurance

It was 1960. He was 22 and in debt for more than $250,000. His wife of three years asked for a separation at the same time.

"The whole world just seemed to go out from under me," Ortega once said describing this period. "I couldn't seem to bring myself back. It took four years. I kept trying and trying and nothing was right. I knew I still had the initiative."

In 1964, he scraped together enough money to build Indian Village in Lupton, Ariz. Although the village burned down a couple of years after it was built, it became the cornerstone of his arts and crafts business.

From there he got the idea of building dome-shaped arts and crafts centers; he constructed two within a year and by 1969 had paid off all of his creditors.

He n...
built a s...
Gallup...
bedroom...

The s...
jewelry...
back...

Ort...
$600,0...
but f...
well...
eve...
ne...
cre...

THE TRUTH WELL TOLD

Ir...pendent

...om Alice

...co's 40-year-old jewelry magnate ...tega (left) takes a few minutes ... 12-hour work day to talk about ...nship in this kachina doll with ...rsmith Alice Sam. Ortega be-

...gan his business career at age ...sold a horse for $50 and bui... ...$500 profit. Today, his expan... ...stores in Texas and Arizon... ...in New Mexico.

...Ortega: millionaire

...ler 'struck go...

...VD
...on his
...nental
...cense
...r-old
...mag-
...'s a

spelling mistake. It should read "GOD."

ORTEGA PUSHED open the glass door of Kristy's Restaurant in Gallup and strode in scuffed cowboy boots toward the car.

He wore black slacks, a white, embroidered shirt — open to mid-chest — and a burgundy sports coat. At 5-foot-9, he is, except for a slightly heavy belly, a trim man, who looks much like actor Earl Holloman of TV's "Police Woman."

As he crossed the parking lot, the dirty wind ruffled his graying hair. He pointed to his initials on the license

plate and laughed. H... consider him somethi... even in a joking manne... backs in his personal... have left Ortega feel... god-like.

"I'VE BEEN DOW... had to reach up to tou... he said. "At one time ... was a bum. I felt, 'M... against me."

It's not that Ortega ... big in business. He h... he's not secure in his ...

Continue...

ONLY 50¢

Clark's Country Music News

Gilbert Ortega

ear he
ore in
l two-
tore.
"great
t for In
ive set

between
he crash
ugh and
d on while
titors get

o that if he
welry busi-
ke a try at

B-12 Tues., Dec. 27, '77 The Arizona Republic

Ortega shooting for country fame

By BILL DONOVAN

GALLUP, N.M. — Can a 41-year-old former "king of Indian jewelry" find happiness in the country music business?

The question may be answered in the next few months, as Gilbert Ortega attempts to launch a career in the music industry.

Ortega, who started from scratch several years ago and built an Indian jewelry business which he sold recently for $4 million, said he decided to cut a country single because he wanted a challenge after divesting himself of most of his Indian jewelry holdings.

SO FAR, SAID Ortega, the response to his first single, "Is It Wrong?", a Warner-McPherson composition, has been gratifying. Trans-American Programming, which operates out of Palm Springs, Cal., and supplies a syndicated daily show to some 154 stations, named the record a "pick hit of the week."

"I'm getting phone calls from all over the country now from disc jockeys who want to know about me and the record," he said. Many of the callers are aware of the Gilbert Ortega name, he said, because of his Indian jewelry business, and ask him if he is the same one.

AGENDA

About 10,000 copies of the single, which was produced in Nashville by Little Richie Johnson, have been mailed to disc jockeys throughout the country. Most have praised the record, but Ortega said he received one post card from a disc jockey who wrote: "Good song, no voice."

IF YOU GO TO a record store, however, and try to buy the single, don't be surprised if the record dealer doesn't have any. Shipments to record dealers are expected to being in the next couple of weeks.

Also planned for the future, said Ortega, is an album that he cut a few months ago in Nashville. The album, entitled "Gilbert Ortega Goes Country," will also include old standards such as "Cold, Cold Heart," and "Send Me the Pillow." It will be on the market in two or three months.

Now that he is out of the Indian jewelry business, Ortega said he plans to spend more time working on his country music career.

"I'VE ALWAYS wanted to do something in country music," he said. "Up until now, I have never really had the time to do much." For several years, however, Ortega did sing in the Gallup area with a local country-western band called Gil Dean and the Westerners.

He already owns one country "record." When his first single came off the assembly line, he sold it to Joe Atkinson — a long-time friend and the Gallup dealer who purchased his jewelry holdings — for $2,000, which, said Ortega, is the highest amount ever paid for a just-released single.

The money actually was the result of a bet placed between Atkinson and Ortega. Atkinson, who did no believe Ortega when he said he would do a countr album, bet him $2,000 that he was just kidding.

Gilbert Ortega returns from Nashville
'The King of Indian Jewelry Goes Country'

Gilbert Ortega records album

By DAVE NORDSTRAND
Tribune Staff Writer

Former Indian jewelry magnate and State Police Board member Gilbert Ortega says he has begun a new career, country and western singing.

Ortega has just returned from Nashville, Tenn., where he recorded his first album, "The King of Indian Jewelry Goes Country," Ortega said.

"This is a very, very serious thing for me. I definitely want to go into it full time," he said.

ORTEGA, WHO sold his Indian jewelry empire in June for roughly $5 million, said his album will be released within the next few weeks.

"We've got a whole national promotional campaign," he said. "It takes so much money, it just can't be a sideline."

Ortega said he began his siging career in high school in Gallup when he played for dances in New Mexico and Arizona in his band, "Gil-Dean and the Westerners."

Ortega spent two weeks in Nashville, he said. And he cut the record with "the top studio peopl

THE "TOP PEOPLE," said Ortega, in on guitar, Charlie McCoy on harmonic on fiddle and "Pig" Robbins on piano.

"Then we filled in with sax and trum Most of the songs on the album ar cluding "Cold, Cold Heart" and "Send said.

The songs are sung in Spanish ar Ortega said he plays a western guitar

"AFTER ALL THIS comes out, w concerts," he said. "Possibly we'll singers, but we want to get me off th

The new record will be available

Ortega said he was looking for a is forbidden from competing with ry stores for two years.

Gov. Jerry Apodaca appointed State Police Board. Before that, governor's Board of Economic D

Horse Traders Join Big Time

From a $50 horse to a $5 million chain of jewelry stores, the business dealings of Gilbert Ortega and Joe Atkinson have evolved.

Wednesday afternoon, Ortega sold his three-state chain of 16 Indian jewelry stores to Atkinson.

The lifelong friends, who grew up together in Lupton, Ariz., and now live in Gallup, finished the deal after nearly five months of negotiations.

Ortega explained the sale saying "The price was right," adding he wants to move on to some other kind of business venture.

Atkinson described the action as being "typical" of Ortega. "Gil works super hard putting something like this together and once it's going and easy to run, he gets rid of it."

Ortega began his business dealings with Atkinson when he was 12 and Atkinson was 8. With "pennies, nickels and dimes" Atkinson bought a horse from Ortega for the price of $50. "It was a good deal for a kid," Atkinson said.

Of the 16 stores involved in the deal, Ortega said they usually make about $200,000 to $300,000 a year each but added that one did $1.25 million in business last year.

A land developer and owner of the Atkinson Trading Co. of Gallup, Atkinson said he wanted to branch out in the Indian jewelry market and that the quality of Ortega's goods was "just what we were looking for."

Atkinson said he plans to merge his wholesale trading outfit with his new stores, get that operation going, and then expanded again. Atkinson said he is particularly interested in expanding along the West Coast.

The stores, located in New Mexico, Arizona and Texas, will retain Ortega's name for about a month, then will assume a variety of titles, each encorporating Atkinson's name.

New Mexico stores included in the purchase are The Oldest House and La Fonda Indian Shop, both in Santa Fe, Gilbert Ortega's in Albuquerque and Top of the World Jewelry Co. located on the Continental Divide near Gallup. Ortega said he will keep his new jewelry store in Gallup.

GILBERT ORTAGA

"King of Indian Jewelry Goes Country

Gilbert Ortega comes from a Spanish immagrant family. His great-grandfather was Santos Ortega who came from Spain to Arizona in the 1880's.

As a youngster, Gilbert was often reminded by his father that Indian Arts and Crafts would be good someday. At the age of ... sold a horse

portion back to his creditors. But there was nothing left to start on elsewhere.

At the end of 1963, Gilbert began working again for the future and worked until he felt the urge to start out on his own again. At this time Gilbert became a partner with his brother. They worked together for six months, then Gilbert decided to go out on his own.

...nce began to show
time when
ore in Lup-
became the
ater succes-
ge in Lupton
third class
few Navajo
hough fire
here were no
and the first
, was replaced
me-type build-

ear's time a
was built in
na. By this time
elry had come
time" and busi-
od. In five years
repaid all hi
nd was completel
t. He opened u
s in New Mexic
and Texas, four
xico, four in A
d two in Texas
factory in Phoen
was built to mar
silversmith supplie
Ortega had o
an silversmith
nd owned 26 b
throughout
tes.
ecoming the
in Indian jew
ided he want
first of lov
sic. Gilbert
e Richie Joh
n agreed to
tional prom
ction. Gil
nd album
abel.

'Indian Jewelry King' Will Write 2 Books

GALLUP (Staff) – Gilbert Ortega, the former "king of Indian jewelry" said Thursday that his next major project will be in the publishing industry.

"I would like to spend the next several months writing a couple of books," he said. The books will center, he added, on his life as a jewelry dealer and how he made a fortune in Indian arts and crafts.

He said he also wanted to write a book on how to get into the Indian jewelry business and some of the pitfalls that persons going into the business should look out for.

"I get people asking me questions like this all the time," Ortega said.

Ortega, who was described by several news writers as the "king of Indian jewelry," sold most of his holdings to Joe Atkinson, a Gallup Indian trader, earlier this week for about $5 million.

Atkinson will receive 14 of Ortega's 16 Indian arts and crafts stores throughout Arizona, New Mexico, and Texas. Ortega said he will keep his two stores in Gallup and continue in the wholesale business, but on a much smaller scale.

"I have no plans on expanding from the two stores, at least not for a while," Ortega said.

He called the sale of most of his holdings the "largest transaction of its type in the country."

"The transaction was so big no one realizes just how big it was," he said. "People just do not acquire that much Indian arts and crafts at one time. all I can say is that Joe has bought himself a monster."

He added that he thought Atkinson had made a good deal and purchased the stores at a time when their value would be increasing substantially in the next couple of years.

"It would not surprise me if these stores were worth $10 million to $12 million in the next couple of years," he said.

When asked why he decided to sell most of his holdings at this time, Ortega said he felt "the price was right."

"Besides, it's been my practice to build a store up and then sell," he added.

He said he thinks that there are still a lot of opportunities for persons to make their fortunes in the indian jewelry business.

"When I got started (in 1964) you could have started out in a shoe box with an investment of about $1,000," he said. "Nowadays a person would have to be willing to put up between $75,000 and $150,000 for a nice retail store."

He added that he even thought a person could even open another indian jewelry store in Gallup, which has more Indian jewelry stores for a town its size in the country.

"It would depend on who the person is," Ortega said. "I know that if I wanted to put a third store here, I am going to make it profitable."

The thing people interested in the Indian jewelry business have to remember, he said, is that "good quality Indian jewelry will always be in demand".

City Roundup

Airport Sites Discussed

GALLUP (Staff) – Members of the Airport Commission heard Thursday hat a site at Carbon Coal would be the best alternate for an airport. But no decision has been made yet on whether to move the facility

Trails Group To Picnic

GALLUP (Staff) – Members of the Zuni ... meet for a picnic at El Morro Nati... at 5 p.m. and those ...

...om page one A-1

Thursday, April 14, 1977

Jeweler 'struck gold'

...ed from Page 1

...is national reputation ...ian jewelry dealer. He

...ings include two jewel- ...allup and land around ...f Course. He owns one ...in Albuquerque's Coron- ...ree in Texas and five in

...MOTEL, restaurant and ...e in Cameron, Ariz. Plans ...new jewelry stores in San ...s Angeles, in Honolulu and ...t Regency Hotel in Chica-

...tega visits his various en- ..., he flies in his personal, ...enger 1976 Cessna 402. ...ga "has arrived" in business. ...rival might entitle the mil- ...o feel a little haughty, a cut ...s peers. He might feel that ..., if the road to the top hadn't ...ough.

...WHEN YOU'VE been down and ...ted and broke, you learn a lit- ...ility, Ortega said, and you don't ...t easily.

...ert Ortega is the fourth genera- ...Ortegas to come from Arizona. ...ther, Max, now 75 and still ac- ...business, was an Indian trader. ...ge 12, Gilbert sold his horse for ...and asked his father what he ...d do with the money. ...ut it into jewelry and rugs." Max ...his son.

...ILBERT BUILT his $50 into a $500 ...fit, he said. "I kind of got a taste of ...business."

After high school in Gallup, Ortega ...ent to work for his brother, Armond, ...Deming. Armond owned the Apache ...illage Trading Post. While working ...here, Ortega decided the business ...was for him, he said.

A few small ventures, then he made ...his first — and nearly his last — big ...time money move.

He leased land from the Navajo Tribe near Navajo, N.M., and borrowed enough money to build and stock a 7,000-square-foot shopping center.

UNFORTUNATELY, he didn't borrow enough to cover the center with fire insurance. And, after flames raced through the development, Ortega was left with a quarter-million-dollar debt. He was 22.

...was the low point in his business ...life began to

At 19, he had been married. "We were separated after I lost everything," he said.

"The whole world just seemed to go from under me. I couldn't seem to bring myself back. It took four years. I kept trying and trying, and nothing was right. I knew I still had the initiative."

IN 1964, FOUR years later, Ortega put together enough money to finance Indian Village at Lupton, Ariz. The village, which later burned, became the backbone of his chain of stores.

He then hit on building dome-shaped stores. He constructed two within a year and paid off his creditors within five years.

Gilbert Ortega stores began sprouting in New Mexico and Arizona. A factory was built in Phoenix to manufacture silversmith supplies.

BUT WHILE HIS business thrived, his marriage withered. Five years ago, he and his wife were divorced. The frustration in his personal life pushed him harder in his professional career, he said.

"I just kind of said a little prayer and was able to keep going and to build more than I ever did before," Ortega said. "I had enough common sense and knowledge to know that you can keep going.

"Adversity is like liquor. If you can't handle it, it will break you. I feel in my business, it has helped me. And, right now, I'm more content in my personal life than ...

He may work from 8 a.m. in his Gallup headquarters, ... the airport, fly to Phoenix, ... store office and return to New Mexico in the morning.

Ortega lives alone in a small, two-bedroom apartment above his new store in Gallup. There is little leisure time.

"Now, 90 per cent of my time is devoted to my business," he said. "My business is my relaxation. My hobby is building stores. I haven't played golf for three years, but I still enjoy life."

"BUT I'M THROUGH pushing, trying to get this deal closed and that deal closed. If it's there, what the hell, I'll take it. Things will fall where they fall."

Increasingly, the thought of getting out of the jewelry business has crossed Ortega's mind. He would like to go into land development.

But then 1977 will be a bumper profit year for him in his business, he said. It will be the feast after the famine.

Last year brought "the great jewelry crash," when thousands of pseudo-artists glutted the Indian jewelry business, he said.

ORTEGA SAID HE lost $600,000 to $700,000, but was big enough and established enough to hold on. Many of his competitors were wiped out.

"You have to be a fighter to stay on top," he said, "but you never have to be cold.

Jewelry firm sold for $5 million

Jewelry czar Gilbert Ortega
Eyes nightclub, land ventures

By DAVE NORDSTRAND
Tribune Staff Writer

New Mexico's Indian jewelry czar, Gilbert Ortega, said today he has sold his three-state chain of jewelry stores for about $5 million.

In all, 16 businesses, including Ortega's store at Coronado Center in Albuquerque, were purchased by Gallup's Joe Atkinson, Ortega's boyhood friend.

ATKINSON, 36, owns Atkinson Trading Co. Inc. of Gallup. Before the purchase, Atkinson owned one large Indian jewelry store and was in the Indian wholesale jewelry business.

"The price was right, so I sold," Ortega said. "This is the biggest deal of its kind in the Indian arts and crafts business anywhere."

Other stores purchased by Atkinson are in Houston, Dallas, Phoenix, Scottsdale, Ariz., Santa Fe, on I-40 near the New Mexico-Arizona line and in Cameron, Ariz., near the Grand Canyon.

A RESTAURANT, motel and supermarket are among the businesses that will go to Atkinson, Ortega said.

He said he will keep his new jewelry store in Gallup.

"As far as the stores go," he said, "I have no partners. The business is something I've built from the ground up. And when you know how good something's been to you, you hate to let it go. But the name of the game is profit."

ORTEGA MIGHT BUILD a chain of nightclubs or develop land, he said. He said he plans to expand his Indian wholesale jewelry business.

"Anything to make money with," he said. "I'm under more pressure now than ever, trying to figure out what I'm going to do."

The contract, said Ortega, forbids him from competing with Atkinson in some areas of the Indian jewelry business for two years. Atkinson said Ortega's name will remain on the stores for an undetermined time.

THE MULTI MILLION-DOLLAR deal began as something of a joke, Ortega said.

"We were in Pal Joey's Restaurant in Gallup," he said, "and Joe was there. I heard him say, 'I need to invest some money.' And I said, 'Hey, why don't you buy my stores out?'"

A few days later, Atkinson's initial

Continued on Page A-9

Ortega

Continued from Page 1

offer was on Ortega's desk, Ortega said. Atkinson said he had sold some real estate and was looking for an investment.

"That's the way we do business," Atkinson said. "Everything's informal. Everything's been figured out on cocktail and dinner napkins before we let the attorneys haggle over it."

THE TWO NEW Mexico businessmen began dealing when Atkinson was 8 and Ortega was 12.

Ortega sold Atkinson a horse named Sandy for $50.

"I told him it was the best horse in the world," Ortega said. "Joe bought it with a bag of nickles and dimes."

Ortega built his $50 into a $500 profit, he said. A train hit and killed his horse, Atkinson said.

"I JUST HOPE none of these stores are close to a railroad track," Atkinson said.

Atkinson said he has already suffered a $150,000 loss in the new deal. Last Tuesday, his newly acquired jewelry store in Cameron, Ariz. burned.

Album cover from "The King of Indian Jewelry Goes Country," 1977.

The King of Indian Jewelry Goes Country

"Mae Axton agreed to hear my demo tape. And she liked it."

Nashville, the country music capital, is a place where dreams come true. Sometimes. Dreams require qualities like talent, good looks, money, connections. And I thought I possessed those elements. Besides, I was accustomed to taking the threads of dreams and weaving them into a tapestry of reality.

I summoned my determination and dug my heels into the project. I spent several months researching country music, working on the songs I wanted to use — practicing. I thought that recording the songs in English and Spanish would be timely. I had worked on the songs and I added some lyrics in Spanish to get some very personal messages across. For example, in *Nobody's Darlin' But Mine,* I lament the loss of my mother, my brothers, and of course, Linda.

I hired someone to translate the songs into Spanish, so one language could flow into the other. Ray Martinez of Gallup worked with me for about three months. We went through hundreds of songs, honing it down to the 12 best suited for me to record. Some were the old country songs I used to sing in high school.

Then, I got in touch with Little Richie Johnson, a promoter, out of Belen, New Mexico. I sent him my demo tape, and he said it was time to go to Nashville. I didn't know how much it was going to cost me, but I knew I wanted to do it.

Little Richie was slick — an energetic fast talker, fast mover. He was determined to introduce me to Mae Axton in Nashville. She was Hoyt Axton's mother. Eventually, I met Hoyt Axton, who wrote Elvis Presley's hit *Heartbreak Hotel.*

As a force in the industry, Mae Axton could get an entertainer the needed publicity to get them noticed — air time on radio stations and appearances on TV shows. She was known for creating legends in the country music business, and I was determined to get her on my side.

In Nashville, we hired a 15-piece backup band, the Nashville Addition, as well as country singer, Janie Frickie, as an accompanying vocalist. There in the studio, I recorded my bilingual selection, for the album to be called *The King of Indian Jewelry Goes Country*. It took 14 days of practicing and recording from 6 o'clock in the morning to well after midnight each day to create the finished product, recording, listening, dubbing, overdubbing.

Little Richie had the demo tape, but he needed Mae Axton's support for this to go any further. Richie made several unsuccessful phone calls. He was told Mae was out or in a meeting, time after time. He continued to leave messages. Finally, his persistence paid off. I wasn't aware that she had intentionally tried to avoid Richie's calls. His reputation in Nashville was less than perfect. When he finally did get through, he tried to convince her to listen to a demo tape of his exciting new talent.

But Mae had a plan to get rid of Little Richie.

"Furnish me with a stretch limo and a check for $1,000, and I'll listen to the tape," she insisted.

She was positive Little Richie couldn't swing a deal like that, and it would get him off her back.

Richie told me what Mae had proposed, and I executed the plan. Richie and I showed up at Mae's office in the limo, and I presented her with my personal check for $1,000, as well as a beautiful piece of Indian jewelry.

Mae was surprised, impressed — and maybe a little embarassed — so she agreed to hear my demo tape. And she liked it.

Afterward, when she felt more comfortable with me, Mae leaned forward and stared at me across the desk. She was bluntly honest when she asked me why I wanted to go into the music business. In my early 40's, to her I seemed too old to start a music career. She said agents looked for young, raw talent, to be molded and fitted to an image.

"What about your Indian arts and crafts business?" she asked. "Do you like what you are doing?"

"Of course," I answered. "I love it."

She made me a deal. If I would go back into the business I loved, she would promote my record and have it played on radio stations, get air time — get me on talk shows. The talk show part created a sudden recurrence of my shyness.

The first single, *Is It Wrong?* hit the top hundred in Billboard and Cash Box — thanks again to Mae Axton. One syndicated program, which operated out of Palm Springs, named it a "Pick Hit of the Week." In Phoenix, *Is It Wrong?* hit number 13.

The other side of the single was *Is This All There Is To A Honky Tonk.*

We produced 10,000 of the 45 rpm singles. I probably invested about $150,000 in my recording venture.

Best of all, though, while the record never went platinum, one record did sell for $2,000. To Joe Atkinson. I delivered it in person.

The album, which came out a few months later, included old standards like *Cold, Cold Heart,* and *Send Me The Pillow.*

When the album was released, I gave Joe an autographed copy. Free.

I kept in touch with Mae Axton. She passed away several years ago, but she was one of the greatest people I've ever known.

You would be surprised at how many records and albums I sold, even though I never went on the road. I was satisfied that I had achieved my goal, a personal accomplishment. I had no intention of going into the music business, but I wanted to make the record, go to Nashville. That was hard work, and it took patience and perseverance. I'm the most "impatient, *patient*" person around. I've been told I'm impatient, but I just want to finish things. If I really were impatient, I wouldn't have tried to make that record.

There was a time when I thought that going to Nashville and recording the album was my greatest accomplishment. I had taken myself out of my comfort zone and attained something that I had dreamed about. Now I look at it as an accomplishment outside the realm of business, as more of a personal achievement — a very satisfying personal achievement.

The King of Indian Jewelry CD
is included with this book.

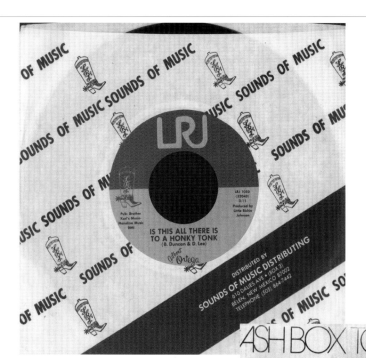

*Gilbert's recording
"Is It Wrong,"
makes
Cashbox Top 100.*

Billboard
Hot Country Singles™

Billboard SPECIAL SURVEY For Week Ending 1/28/78

© Copyright 1978, Billboard Publications, Inc. No part of this publication may be reproduced, stored in a retrieval system, or transmitted, in any form or by any means, electronic, mechanical, photocopying, recording, or otherwise, without the prior written permission of the publisher.

★ STAR PERFORMER—Singles registering greatest proportionate upward progress this week.

This Week	Last Week	Weeks on Chart	TITLE—Artist (Writer), Label & Number (Dist. Label) (Publisher, Licensee)
1	3	9	OUT OF MY HEAD AND BACK IN MY BED—Loretta Lynn (P. Forman), MCA 40832 (Hello Darlin' SESAC)
2	1	11	WHAT A DIFFERENCE YOU MADE IN MY LIFE—Ronnie Milsap (A. Jordan), RCA 11146 (Chess, ASCAP)
★	7	9	YOU'RE THE ONE—Oakridge Boys (B. Morrison), ABC/Dot 17732 (Glenwood/Arcane, ASCAP)
★	6	9	TO DADDY—Emmylou Harris (D. Parton), Warner Bros. 8498 (Owepar, BMI)
5	4	14	MIDDLE AGE CRAZY—Jerry Lee Lewis (S. Throckmorton), Mercury 55011 (Tree, BMI)
★	9	8	I JUST WISH YOU WERE SOMEONE I LOVE—Larry Gatlin (L. Gatlin), Monument 234 (Phonogram) (First Generation, BMI)
★	13	7	DON'T BREAK THE HEART THAT LOVES YOU—Margo Smith (B. Davis, T. Murry), Warner Bros. 8508 (Gyrol, ASCAP)
8	2	11	MY WAY—Elvis Presley (Anka, Revaux, Francois), RCA 11165 (Spanka, BMI)
9	5	13	TAKE THIS JOB AND SHOVE IT/COLORADO COOL AID—Johnny Paycheck (D. Coe), Epic 8-50469 (Warner Tamerlane, BMI)
10	11	11	SOMETHING TO BRAG ABOUT—Mary Kay Place (B. Braddock), Columbia 3-10644 (Tree, BMI)
★	17	6	WHAT DID I PROMISE HER LAST NIGHT—Mel Tillis (B. McCowen, W. Walker), MCA 40836 (Sawgrass, BMI)
12	8	12	LONELY STREET—Rex Allen Jr. (K. Sowder, C. Belew, W. Stevenson), Warner Bros. 8487 (Four Star, BMI)
★	18	6	WOMAN TO WOMAN—Barbara Mandrell (J. Banks, E. Marion, H. Thigpen), ABC/Dot 17736 (East Memphis, BMI)
14	15	9	MAY THE FORCE BE WITH YOU—Tom T. Hall (T.T. Hall), RCA 11158 (Halmote, BMI)
★	20	9	I DON'T NEED A THING AT ALL—Gene Watson (L. Allen), Capitol 4513 (Jim Allen)
★	21	5	DO I LOVE YOU (Yes In Every Way)—Donna Fargo (P. Anka, M. Pigat, Y. Desaca, A. Leroux, M. Petay) (Spanka, ASCAP) Warner Bros. 8509
17	10	12	THE FIRST TIME—Billy "Crash" Craddock (J. Adrian), ABC/Dot 17729 (Pick-A-Hit, BMI)
18	19	5	SOME I WROTE—Statler Brothers (D. Reid, H. Reid), Mercury 55013 (Cowboy, BMI)
19	14	12	STANDARD LIE NUMBER ONE—Stella Parton (D. Wilson), Elektra 45437 (Tree, BMI)
★	36	2	MAMAS DON'T LET YOUR BABIES GROW UP TO BE COWBOYS/I CAN GET OFF ON YOU—Waylon & Willie (E. Bruce, P. Bruce)/(W. Nelson, W. Jennings), RCA 11198 (Tree/Sugarplum, BMI)/(Willie Nelson/Waylon Jennings)
21	23	8	I PROMISED HER A RAINBOW—Bobby Borchers (R. Bourke), Playboy 85823 (Epic) (Chappell, ASCAP)
★	31	6	I LOVE YOU, I LOVE YOU, I LOVE YOU—Ronnie McDowell (R. McDowell), Scorpion 149 (GRT) (Brim, SESAC)
★	30	6	SHINE ON ME (The Sun Still Shines When It Rains)—John Wesley Ryles (T. Skinner, J. Wallace), RCA 17732 (Naver Joe Marsel, BMI)
★	29	7	SHAKE ME I RATTLE—Cristy Lane (H. Hackady, C. Nayne), LS 149 (GRT) (Regent BMI)
25	25	11	HOLD TIGHT—Kenny Starr (D. Gates), MCA 40837 (Kipahulu, ASCAP)
26	26	9	WE GOT LOVE—Lynn Anderson (L. Keith, S. Pippin, H. Furniss, R. Tison), Columbia 3-10650 (Tree, BMI)
★	32	7	GOD MADE LOVE—Mel McDaniel (McDaniel, Lindie, MacKay, Pollard), Capitol 2855 (Combine, BMI Music City, ASCAP)
★	33	7	TWO DOORS DOWN—Zella Lehr (D. Parton), RCA 11174 (Owepar, BMI)
★	35	8	ANGEL OF THE MORNING—Melba Montgomery (C. Taylor), United Artists 1115 (Blackwood, BMI)
★	37	6	YOU KNOW WHAT—Jerry Reed & Seidina (J. Hubbard), RCA 11164 (Vector BMI)
★	40	5	BARTENDER BLUES—George Jones (J. Taylor), Country Road, EMI Four 0485
32	22	10	HOW CAN I LEAVE YOU AGAIN—John Denver (J. Denver), RCA 11173 (Cherry Lane ASCAP)
33	16	17	COME TO ME—Ronnie Head (G. Price), ABC/Dot 17722 (Acoustic Longstreet, BMI)

This Week	Last Week	Weeks on Chart	TITLE—Artist (Writer), Label & Number (Dist. Label) (Publisher, Licensee)
★	41	6	I'VE BEEN LOVED—Cates Sisters (B. Lewis), Caprice 2041 (Sound ASCAP)
★	56	3	IF I HAD A CHEATING HEART—Mel Street (W. Holyfield, A. Turney), Polydor 14448 (Maplehill/Vogue, BMI)
37	38	8	ALWAYS LOVIN' HER MAN—Dale McBride (H. Kinman), Con Brio 127 (NSD) (Con Brio, BMI)
★	46	6	THE LONGEST WALK—Mary K. Miller (E. Polop, F. Spielman), Inergi 304 (NSD) (Advanced) ASCAP
★	58	3	RUNNING KIND—Merle Haggard (M. Haggard), Capitol 4525 (Shadetree, BMI)
40	42	8	I'VE CRIED (The Blues Right Out Of My Eyes)—Crystal Gayle (L. Lynn), MCA 40837 (Sure Fire, BMI)
41	24	10	YOU AND ME ALONE—David Rogers (R. Klang, D. Plimmer), Republic 011 (Singletree, BMI)
★	65	3	LONELY HEARTS CLUB—Billie Jo Spears (Butler, Bowling, Simmons), United Artists 1127 (ATV/Blackwood, BMI)
43	12	14	COME A LITTLE BIT CLOSER—Johnny Duncan (with Janie Fricke) (Boyce, Hart, Farrell), Columbia 310634 (Morris, BMI)
44	44	8	WHAT KIND OF FOOL (Do You Think I Am)—Eddie Middleton (R. Whitley), Cleveland International 8-50481 (Epic) (Low Twi, BMI)
★	55	6	IT DOESN'T MATTER ANYMORE—R.C. Bannon (P. Anka), Columbia 3-10655 (Spanka, BMI)
★	61	5	BEDROOM EYES—Don Drumm (R. Hillburn), Churchill 7704 (Zoobe, ASCAP)
47	27	10	THINK ABOUT ME—Freddy Fender (G. Latimar), ABC/Dot 17730 (Crazy Cajun, BMI)
★	66	2	YES MA'AM—Tommy Overstreet (S. Throckmorton), ABC/Dot 17737 (Tree, BMI)
49	28	16	HERE YOU COME AGAIN—Dolly Parton (B. Mann, C. Weil), RCA 11123 (Screen Gems EMI, Summerhill Songs, BMI)
50	48	13	I JUST WANT TO BE YOUR EVERYTHING—Connie Smith (B. Gibb), Monument 45231 (Stigwood, BMI)
51	52	7	THROWIN' MEMORIES ON THE FIRE—Cal Smith (B. Bond), MCA 40839 (Stone Porch, BMI)
★	62	5	FEELIN' BETTER—Hank Williams Jr. (H. Williams Jr.), (Bocephus, BMI), Warner Bros. 8507
53	43	12	MISTER D.J.—T. G. Sheppard (G. France, B. House) Warner/Curb 58490 (Pointed Star BMI, Joe, ASCAP)
54	39	14	I'M KNEE DEEP IN LOVING YOU—Dave & Sugar (S. Throckmorton), RCA 11141 (Tree, BMI)
55	59	6	AFRAID YOU'D COME BACK—Kenny Price (D. Kirby), MRC 1007 (Tree, BMI)
56	45	14	BABY, LAST NIGHT MADE MY DAY—Susie Allanson (E. Springfield), Warner/Curb KG-1 (House of Gold, BMI)
57	50	8	GEORGIA KEEPS PULLING ON MY RING—Conway Twitty (D. Wilkins, T. Marshall), MCA 40805 (Emerald Isle/Battleground, BMI)
58	60	6	IT STARTED ALL OVER AGAIN—David Houston (S. Miele, G. Paxton, K. Lusk), Starday 172 (Gusto) (Garpax, ASCAP/Raysey, SESAC)
59	49	9	GOD MUST HAVE BLESSED AMERICA—Glen Campbell (A. Toussaint), Capitol 4515 (Warner Tamerlane, Marsaint BMI)
★	86	2	WALK RIGHT BACK—Anne Murray (S. Curtis), Capitol 4527 (Warner Tamerlane, BMI)
61	47	13	CHAINS OF LOVE—Mickey Gilley (A. Nugetre), Playboy 8561 (Belinda Unichappell, BMI)
★	NEW ENTRY		RETURN TO ME—Marty Robbins (C. Lombardo, D. DiMinno), Columbia 10673 (Southern, ASCAP)
★	NEW ENTRY		SOFT LIGHTS AND HARD COUNTRY MUSIC—Moe Bandy (S. Shafer), Columbia 3-10671 (Acuff Rose, BMI)
64	64	8	LEONA—Johnny Russell (H. Hall), RCA 11160 (No Exit, BMI)
65	71	5	MOUNTAIN MUSIC—Porter Wagoner (D. Parton), Owepar, BMI) RCA 11186
★	77	5	DOWN THE ROADS OF DADDY'S DREAMS—Darrell McCall (M. Sherrill, D. Goodman), (High Ball, BMI) Columbia 10653

This Week	Last Week	Weeks on Chart	TITLE—Artist (Writer), Label & Number (Dist. Label) (Publisher, Licensee)
★	78	3	CARLENA AND JOSE GOMEZ—Billy Walker (J. Jackson, B. Damron), MRC 1009 (Metamoros, BMI)
69	72	5	IF IF EVER COME BACK—Pal Rakes (P. Rakes, R. Faith), (Dusty Roads/Gallico, BMI), Warner Bros. 8506
★	80	3	CRY, CRY DARLING—Glenn Barber (J. Newman, J. D. Miller), Groovy 103 (NSD) (Acuff Rose, BMI)
71	69	7	ANGELINE—Mundo Earwood (M. Earwood, D. Heard), True III (World Wide) (Music Of The Times, BMI)
★	85	2	IT STARTED ALL OVER AGAIN—Vern Gosdin (S. Miele, G. Paxton, K. Lusk), Elektra 4541 (Garpax, ASCAP/Raysey, SESAC)
★	88	2	RED HOT MEMORY—Kenny Dale (W. W. Wimberly), Capitol 4528 (Publicare, ASCAP)
★	NEW ENTRY		I'M WAY AHEAD OF YOU—Bill Anderson & Mary Lou Turner (C. Putman, S. Throckmorton), MCA 40852 (Tree, BMI)
75	54	13	SAVIN' THIS LOVE FOR YOU—Johnny Rodriguez (L. Hargrove), Mercury 55012 (Window, BMI)
★	87	2	SO GOOD, SO RARE, SO FINE—Freddie Hart (S. Stone, H. Shannon), Capitol 4530 (ATV/Welbeck, ASCAP)
★	92	2	DEEPER WATER—Brenda Kay Perry (J. McBee), MRC 1010 (Millstone, BMI)
★	NEW ENTRY		MUSIC IS MY WOMAN—Don King (S. Summer), Con Brio 129 (NSD) (Con Brio, BMI)
79	57	8	I LIKE TO BE WITH YOU—Ronnie Sessions (B. Wood, J. Christopher), MCA 40831 (Unichappell/Chriswood, BMI)
★	90	2	HONKY TONK TOYS—A. L. "Doodle" Owens (A. L. "Doodle" Owens, J. Vowell), Raindrop 10 (Unichappell, BMI)
81	79	7	SOMETIMES I DO/HALF MY HEART'S IN TEXAS—Ernest Tubb (J. Seely/L. Hargrove), First Generation 001 (Tree, BMI/Window/Beachwood, BMI)
★	NEW ENTRY		EVERYBODY LOVES A RAIN SONG—B.J. Thomas (M. James, C. Moman), MCA 40854 (Screen Gems EMI/Baby Chick/Stratton House, BMI)
83	63	8	I'VE GOT A FEELIN' (Somebody's Stealin')—John Anderson (J. Anderson, M. Garvin, E. James), Warner Brothers 8480 (Al Gallico, BMI/Easy Listening, ASCAP)
84	51	12	I'LL PROMISE YOU TOMORROW—Jerry Wallace (F. Stanton, S. Shingler, A. Badale), BMA 7005 (Edwin R. Morris/Chip 'n' Dale, ASCAP)
85	53	13	I'LL GET OVER YOU—Nick Nixon (B. Peters), Mercury 55010 (Shelby Singleton, BMI)
86	67	15	SWEET MUSIC MAN—Kenny Rogers (K. Rogers), United Artists 1095 (Jolly Rogers, ASCAP)
★	NEW ENTRY		SMOKE! SMOKE! SMOKE! (That Cigarette)—Tom Bresh (M. Travis, T. Williams), ABC/Dot 17738 (Belinda, BMI)
88	93	5	JAMBALAYA (On The Bayou)—Sashia & Serge (H. Williams), (Rose, BMI), ABC/Hickory 54020
89	89	2	SWEET COUNTRY GIRL—Mack Sanders (M. Sanders), Pilot 101 (Shema, ASCAP)
★	NEW ENTRY		THE FARMER'S SONG (We Ain't Gonna Work For Peanuts)/DIRT FARMING MAN—Joel Mathis (J. Duncan, J. Gibson/J. Duncan), Soundwaves 4562 (NSD) (Hitkit, BMI/Hitkit, BMI)
91	76	8	THE WRONG SIDE OF THE RAINBOW—Jim Chesnut (S. Shafer), ABC/Hickory 54021 (Acuff Rose, BMI)
92	NEW ENTRY		IS IT WRONG—Gilbert Ortega (W. McPherson), LRI 1050 (Sounds of Music) (Not Available)
93	95	3	DON'T LET THE FLAME BURN OUT—Rita Remington (J. DeShannon), Plantation 167 (Halwill/Plain And Simple, ASCAP)
94	94	3	I LOVE HOW YOU LOVE ME—Joni Lee (B. Mann, L. Kolber), (Screen Gems EMI, BMI), MCA 40826
95	97	2	TENNESSEE—Ray Sanders (R. Klang, D. Plimmer) Republic 013 (Singletree, BMI)
96	96	5	DON'T WORRY ('Bout Me)—Glenda Griffith (M. Robbins), (Noma/Presley, BMI), Ariola America 7680
97	NEW ENTRY		TAKE ME TO BED—Jeannie Seely (H. Cochran, G. Martin), Columbia 3-10664 (Tree, BMI)
98	NEW ENTRY		MR. SANDMAN—Tommy O'Day (P. Ballard), Nu Trad 916 (WIG) Edwin H. Morris, ASCAP)
99	NEW ENTRY		LOVESICK BLUES—Jim Owen & The Drifting Cowboys

Gilbert's recording makes Billboard's Hot Country Singles

Gilbert at Christmas, 1979 with daughters
Renée, Desirée and Gayle.

Gilbert entertains
at an opening
in the 1980s.

Tanya Tucker, Gilbert, Mae Axton at Galleria
opening, 1991.

Max Ortega, Sr., Lupton, Arizona mid 1970s.

Loss Passes Through Again

I needed more quality time with Dad, too. His health was failing. In his 70's now, he wouldn't go to the doctor. He was stubborn that way. He had lost Mom and Dewey and Aggie. I guess he had lost some of his will to live. I tried to see him more often. He told me how proud he was of my accomplishments. I was glad that he had witnessed them, knowing that he and Mom had given me the ability to succeed.

It wasn't long before he quietly passed away there in Lupton, on his own terms, and at home in the trailer on January 21, 1979.

Even though I had been expecting it, the news was a crushing blow. With Dad gone, I felt terribly alone. All my success and money couldn't soothe the loss of my father.

After Dad's passing, our family would have almost 20 years without death. In 1998, we lost my brother Maxie to cancer. He was only 65, still a vibrant and successful businessman.

The Valley of Sun and Silver

*"Developing more sophisticated stores with museum-quality merchandise
gave me an edge."*

With another year or so left in my noncompete clause with Joe, I wasn't
sure what I was going to do — "noncompete" was a foreign concept to me. I
worked the Gallup wholesale store and continued to live in the apartment
above it. By then the kids were all out of school, so I sold the house in town,
and Linda took the ranch.

I began thinking of the business on a different level and reflected on
my whirlwind of business endeavors of the past several years. Looking back, I
would never have put a store in Dallas or Houston — even if they gave me
free rent, free merchandise, I still wouldn't do it. It's funny how your mind
changes, how experiences change you, create new realizations. At the time,
nothing would have stopped me from opening in Dallas and Houston. When
we did the jewelry shows there during the boom, we could take in $12,000 in
two days. Those successes fueled my desire to open the Texas stores, especially
when everyone would ask, "When are you coming back," or say "You should
have a store here."

Also, I realized that I didn't want small stores like the Oldest House in
Santa Fe. That would make a better "mom-and-pop" gift shop.

Now that I wasn't hopping from store to store, I hardly used my plane
anymore, except to fly to Phoenix and check on the Hyatt. The more I stud-
ied the Phoenix area, the more appealing it became, especially understanding
Arizona's number one industry — tourism.

In late 1979, I moved to Phoenix. Joe Atkinson still had a couple of
locations in Scottsdale, so he let me have a 400-square foot store on Main
Street in Old Town. It had been a jewelry store and sat next to a stamp collecting shop, down the street from the Kiva Theater. It already had showcases,
so I used them. I just wanted to get into business again. He still owed me
some money, so we worked out our own unique deal — sort of a "I bought,

he bought" kind of thing. He also had the store on the corner of Brown and First Avenue in Old Town. I rolled that into the deal.

Joe was more devoted to Cameron.

I really think Joe bought all my stores just to get Cameron. Ultimately, that was the one he kept and still owns today. He does an incredible amount of business there. It is a fabulous place and it sees zillions of Grand Canyon visitors. For many years, Joe held an annual collectors' auction there in the fall. After my album came out, I performed at one of his auctions. I think he wanted a return on that $2,000 investment in my record.

Shortly after that, I sold my wholesale business in Gallup to Mohammed Ayesh, including the building with the upstairs apartment, allowing the new owner to continue using my name. He listened and learned and realized that I could teach him more about the business.

My plane just sat at the Gallup airport, so I finally sold it, too. Then, I bought a cream-colored Rolls Royce — an updated version of the one from my Richie Rich comic book days. When I drove it down the long driveway to my Paradise Valley home for the first time, I glanced at the old Navajo wagon sitting under the tree. What a contrast. The car reflected my business success, while the wagon echoed my simple beginning.

And Scottsdale presented me with other contrasts. I started noticing what the fine jewelry stores did. I wondered, "Why can't I do this with Indian jewelry?" I observed how the spotlights hit the showcases and made the diamonds glisten. Silver could glisten. I could carry finer lines of jewelry. Funny, I had always been so worried about the electric bill, that I had avoided using expensive lighting. That's probably a throwback to Armand's lectures at Gage. I had to get over that. This was a new era. Sometimes you have to rid your mind of preconceived notions and proceed on instinct and imagination.

As I began improving the Scottsdale stores, I envisioned a more sophisticated, elegant look with beautiful lighting. I created finer showcases and fixtures. It was time to move away from the trading post look of the '60s and '70s on the highways or in Gallup.

In 1980, I started opening more stores in the Phoenix area again at a fast pace: Park Central and Chris Town Mall, Sun City, Carefree, Old Town Scottsdale. Then around 1982 came Lincoln Village, Hilton Village, the Borgata and more. Behind the scenes, I began buying commercial real estate in downtown Scottsdale — a little at a time. Then on Fifth Avenue in Scottsdale, I leased six stores in record time. People would ask me, "Why did you open six stores on Fifth Avenue?"

Because I know tourists. Tourists love to go in every door. That's why I went against the rules and put stores in close proximity to one another. I knew it would work. If I didn't catch them in the first store, I'd catch them in the second and so on. Would other retailers do that? No. But I know the tourist industry.

Scottsdale is a thriving tourist mecca, especially from February through April, when the weather is great. Baseball's spring training draws huge crowds. Resorts, golf courses, restaurants and shopping lure tourists by the thousands. I liked the shoppers, and I wanted them in my stores.

By 1986, I had a big slice of the Scottsdale tourist pie.

With many members of my family in the same business, I needed a unique identity. Everyone was using the Ortega name. When I began expanding in Scottsdale, I had a logo created that blended my first and last name together, so my stores could stand out. And I did a lot of advertising and promotion. It worked, because now many people ask, "Is there really a Gilbert Ortega?" They assume it's a brand name. But that lets me know that my name is recognized and identifies my company.

As often happens, the business changed and shifted. I closed the original mall stores and the Sun City location and concentrated my efforts in Scottsdale.

In December, 1991, I opened a 12,000 square foot store at the Scottsdale Galleria. The Galleria received a lot of hype and everyone had great expectations for it, thinking it would become the equivalent of Rodeo Drive. My store was gorgeous, with a jewelry department, an art gallery, a mezzanine-level Navajo rug room, as well as upscale clothing and smaller boutiques within the larger store.

But the Galleria was doomed — it never created the stir that developers had expected for the high-end venue. In spite of the Galleria's problems, my store accomplished a new look, a sophisticated concept in merchandising and presenting Native American arts and crafts in a museum-like setting.

Then the remodeling and expansion of Scottsdale Fashion Square started. That would alter the retail focus. With the mall extending over Camelback Road and with a south wing showcasing Nordstrom, I predicted that nearby business on Fifth Avenue would change. So I began selling my locations one at a time until all I had left was the big store on the corner of Fifth Avenue and Scottsdale Road. This time my "tourist-in-every-door" theory came back to bite me. Each time I sold off a location, anticipating a rise in sales, I found instead that my business in the existing stores didn't increase by one dime — the shoppers were strolling through those other doors just like they always had. And Fifth Avenue, which had once been the retail hot spot, the tourist haven of Scottsdale, had slowed down.

The business had shifted to Old Town. There is more diversity there — unique shops with western and southwest flavor, and restaurants. It's quite charming, and tourists enjoy themselves. What we have in Old Town is an exact opposite of the homogenized, cookie-cutter stores that tourists see in the malls across the country. Tourism is Arizona's peak industry. Aside from golfers, about 35 percent say sightseeing is their favorite activity, and nearly 25 percent claim shopping. Those are my kind of tourists.

The Native American art business has become mainstream. There's more Indian jewelry sold now than ever in history — also more pottery, rugs, baskets. However, there are more retailers in the mix, too. In Old Scottsdale, it used to be the McGees, the Atkinsons, and a few others.

It's difficult for me to remember the exact chronological order of everything I've done in Scottsdale, all the stores. I've never kept track of things that way because I didn't have goals set on a timetable. Whenever something came along that I wanted to try, I jumped at the opportunity — and continue to do so. I think we create our own business climate. And that climate changes — we have to keep up with the times. We have to look at the big picture and see into the distance, the future. It's as though a retailer has to develop a sixth sense, a finely tuned instinct for what's just ahead. That's another reason why I never counted on business plans or pro formas. If you have a pro forma, take a good look at it, then tear it up, because your business will never turn out that way. It usually doesn't even come close — you can't predict.

But if you want to start something, finish it. Just finish it, some way, somehow.

Throughout my career, I've always asked people's advice. It's a great communication skill. If you ask someone's advice, they open up to you. Pretty soon you're solving a problem or creating a new concept, establishing or solidifying a relationship. And if you're nice to people, they will do anything for you. As my mom used to say, "It's nice to be important. But it's more important to be nice."

In a discussion with a business professional whose opinion I respect, I fielded some thoughts I was exploring. Why have all these small stores scattered around? I'd rather have five good stores — preferably where I owned the real estate, several key pieces in Old Town Scottsdale, and one location on Fifth Avenue. We sat in my office at the store on the south side of Main Street in Old Town. I had bought that building years earlier, and added offices, and a large vault to handle all incoming inventory for distribution to the other stores. Later, when I bought the property on the northeast corner of Scottsdale Road and Main Street, I had planned a building which would hold several small stores that I could rent out to other retailers, like I had done with the old Trader Vic's location on Fifth Avenue.

When I told him I wanted to build 10,000–12,000 square foot stores — my own buildings, on my own property — he said it would cost a fortune. The corner of Main Street and Scottsdale Road would become my primary goal. When I bought the corner, it was Whitey's gas station. Now I created an image of the store in my mind. I could visualize it, picture where the showcases would be placed, where the cash register would sit. It had to flow and be comfortable.

It took about five years to complete this vision, to create a high-end museum-quality, retail concept — in a building that is a showplace itself, where rugged stone, solid stucco and heavy wooden *vigas*, or beams, grace the exterior. Inside, a spectacular metal chandelier, designed by a Native American artisan hangs from the high vaulted ceiling. A sea of showcases and multi-level displays presents some of the finest work by Native American artisans of the southwest. I love rare and beautiful things, too — especially old baskets.

It was in January of 1998, that the museum gallery opened. We held a gala event with ribbon cuttings and a reception with local dignitaries. The family of the late Scottsdale Mayor Herb Drinkwater attended as did former Governor Rose Mofford, and country singer, Tanya Tucker, as well as many close relatives and business associates.

The museum gallery is like having five stores in one.

And the museum felt like a breakthrough — a great accomplishment. To balance the business coverage even more, I decided to open a location at Scottsdale Fashion Square. I negotiated a lease with Westcor and got started on the design and layout.

In June of 1999, I was at Koshari, the mall store, directing design and merchandising, looking forward to opening day. Then I received a horrible phone call. The Old Town store, on the corner of Brown and First, had burst into flames. The sales crew managed to race out and call 911. Fortunately, they were safe. In the five minutes it took me to speed over there from the mall, the old western building had become completely engulfed in fire, and smoke spewed into the downtown sky. Firefighters worked frantically. The air conditioning unit on the roof burst through and seemingly exploded in the center of the store. It was hopeless. I watched helplessly as it burned to the ground. I was devastated at the loss of priceless pottery, kachinas, jewelry, rugs — irreplaceable works I had spent years collecting.

Fire investigators later discovered that the blaze was sparked by some old wiring, and those sparks fed into an inferno that raced through and leveled the entire building.

I just couldn't believe this had happened. It was like a terrible nightmare. My store — every inch of it jammed with beautiful merchandise — had been reduced to a pile of smoldering coals. I didn't think things like this could happen to me anymore. It was gut-wrenching.

But I had to deal with it. At least this time I had insurance. And I had to rebuild.

It took about a year and a half to complete, and the building is definitely an asset to Old Town. The gallery opened in 2001, and it is larger than the museum store, including a second level for unique southwest furnishings. So, out of the destruction has come something great.

I could put ten of my former stores into this new gallery. Yet people still wonder why I don't have 20 or 30 stores anymore. The large stores exceed my expectations from any number of small stores, without a doubt. And the real estate has created another form of investment.

Competition is tough, though. Developing more sophisticated stores with museum-quality merchandise has given me an edge. For example, I now sell Navajo rugs in the range of $30,000-$75,000, and an exquisite piece of Pueblo pottery can sell for as much as $100,000. I am passionate about showcasing the finest collectible work of our southwest Native American artisans.

And I wouldn't trade Scottsdale for any place in the world.

Beginning in 1980, Gilbert starts opening locations, always improving.

One of the first Scottsdale locations on Main Street in Old Town, 1980.

The same Main Street location – years later.

A look at the changes in the Fifth Avenue and Scottsdale Road location —
from 1980 to the present.

Gilbert,
Max, Jr. and
Bruce Babbitt, Governor of Arizona
from 1978-1986.

Gilbert with Rose Mofford,
Governor of Arizona from 1988-1991.

From Left: sculptor John Soderberg, Gilbert and cowboy artist John Hampton (founder of Cowboy Artists of America) at gallery opening in the mid-1980s.

Gilbert with sister Esther André at store opening, 1986.

Gilbert and Native American artist Robert Redbird at a Fifth Avenue gallery opening, 1990.

From left: Sandra McCarrell, Gilbert's niece;
Peri Maestas, employee; Navajo artist R.C.
Gorman; Desirée Ortega, Violet Etsitty,
employee; Bonnie Nelson, Gilbert's niece;
Marisella Gutierrez, employee and
Sandy Wiltcher, employee.

Gilbert and cousin Frances Olguin.

Gilbert with Aunt Margie Gunnels, 1980.

*Danny Medina, Scottsdale <u>Art Talk</u> publisher, Gilbert and
artist Carlos Lopez at Ortega gallery opening at the Borgata.*

A view of the Galleria store on opening night, 1991.

Reminiscing

"Let me teach you what I've spent a lifetime learning."

The galleries have been a great accomplishment for me. When I reflect on my business life, sometimes I consider that triangular store in Lupton as my greatest accomplishment. Then, racing through the boom years like a "Turquoise Tornado" gave me great business momentum. And going to Nashville and recording was something apart from my mainstream of activity. They were all great accomplishments.

Of course, I have regrets and failures. But those pushed me to take a positive attitude and forced me into a different mode. All the failures I had were just steps toward success.

But business was tough. People don't understand what a self-made man goes through. You have to consider every possible scenario when you are in retail. There's no way of knowing what the future holds. You have to keep looking at the big picture, always analyzing.

Because of what Armand and I went through, we are very perceptive. We know the domino effect on things — most people don't understand that. They think about doing something, but they don't know how. They can't envision or execute an idea properly.

If you really dig in and want to succeed, you can. It takes tenacity.

There's no difference between me or any man walking down the street. Most people want to work 35 hours a week — get off at noon Friday, go play golf. For about 25 years, I worked 12 hours a day. If you multiply 12 x 7, you get 72 hours. Say I pay myself for 35 hours. In reality, I actually doubled my income, but I learned to live on the 35-hour income, and therefore invested the remaining income/work into my business. When you do that, everything starts to multiply. I put in more hours and worked harder. I just kept thinking I was putting that money away. I was ready to go. Money comes — you've got to want it.

Whoever works the hardest, gets the most. It's all common sense. If you come in late, leave early, you're not going to achieve as much. It's not that the successful person is smarter or born a genius. It's having the passion to want to do something — and actually doing it. If you've got it inside of you, you're going to make it.

The more you have on your side, the further you get — if you want to.

And starting with nothing doesn't matter.

People say you can't do that today, but you can. You can open a hot dog stand, for example, some place where there's a little traffic, and if you're not afraid to work. At first it might be a little tough, but it's a living. Then, maybe something else will come along to raise the bar. There's always an opportunity for a "mom-and-pop" operation. Always. It depends on you. It depends on the people behind the wheel. There are a lot of people who make a good living in business for themselves — maybe don't get rich, but they're not out to get rich.

Many people don't know what it takes to be successful in the retail business. Making a business succeed requires a clear understanding of the percentages. Should you allow three percent for advertising, or one percent? How much merchandise should you sell per square foot of space?

Different equations work differently at various times. There's no single equation. I had to learn it the hard way. In retail, you have to merchandise every square foot of your location, and continue to turn that merchandise. You can't do yourself justice unless you merchandise to the maximum — with inventory that sells, that turns. The overhead is so high that unless you're doing a huge volume, you can't make it on low-priced merchandise in a gift shop anymore.

To venture into small business takes creative, independent thinking, passion and perseverance. It's a personal adventure.

In spite of my business successes, I'm still very shy. I overcame my stuttering by singing, but shyness still wells up in me. Even now, sometimes I don't make a phone call that I should make — the shyness holds me back. I think maybe I won't know what to say. Shyness stifles me sometimes when I go to introduce someone — even if I've known them my whole life. It's as though I'm stopped cold and can't even remember their name.

A lot of times I have a hard time finding the right words to say. In retrospect, I sometimes wish I had gone to college — a business school, of course — and maybe that environment would have taught me to express myself better.

But I'm not a good listener, either.

And I hold a lot inside. Though I ask for advice, I don't ask for help. I try not to show any weakness. I should reveal more of my feelings.

For some reason, my personal life has always been horrible. I could never get that right. I guess you can't have it all. You have to give up something. For me it was my personal life.

Now it is my health.

I never expected diabetes to do so much damage. I found out I was a diabetic in 1993, when I had a serious heart attack that resulted in six bypasses. It took time to recover, and family members came to my aid, especially my neice, Sandy McCarrell. But I was determined not to let it stop me.

Diabetes is very prevalent in my family and I don't think people know enough about it. I don't really understand it either. But its complications have their grasp on me, and I am dealing with my mortality.

Though I still go to work every day, I spend more time at home than I used to. Some mornings I stand on my front porch and soak up the sun and enjoy the mild breeze as the day comes to life. I watch for cottontail rabbits to hop across the grass, or a covey of Gambel quail to parade along the lengthy driveway.

When I look toward the old Navajo wagon across the yard under the mesquite tree, I reflect, reminisce, and remember. I can close my eyes and picture Lupton — feel the fierce icy winds, smell the piñon smoke in the air, visualize the rugged reservation landscape, hear the basketball pounding on our dirt court, taste Mom's morning coffee.

I treasure those memories.

And I smile at my simple childhood wish to have an old Navajo wagon and two horses, thinking that with them I would be on top of the world.

A view of the Museum Gallery on the corner of Scottsdale Road and Main Street.

New gallery opens in 2001 on the corner of First Avenue and Brown in Old Town.

Ribbon cutting for grand opening of Gilbert Ortega Something Different, 2001 From left: Phil Carlson, President of Scottsdale Chamber of Commerce; Mary Manross, Mayor of Scottsdale; Renée; Gayle; Desirée; David Ortega, Architect; and Bernie Blaustein.

Gilbert greets guests at gallery opening.

Family celebrates gallery opening From left: Desirée, Gayle, Renée, Linda and Gilbert, Jr.

Radio personality and long-time customer Paul Harvey and Gilbert, 2003.

Paul Harvey visits with Gilbert, Jr. at the Museum Gallery, 2005.

In the vault, father and son admire a piece of Santa Clara pottery, 2003.

Turquoise and Silver Sunset

It seems that I am living the final chapter of my life. Though the ravages of diabetes have taken their toll on my body, my spirit and my willpower remain strong. I don't want to give up.

Though I thought I could continue to defy the odds, I've been wrestling with my mortality for nearly a year — not believing the inevitable would arrive. Even when the doctor told me there was nothing more to be done, I wasn't expecting it. It's hard for me to accept. I don't want to believe I'm dying. I don't want to go.

Even though I'm not ready, God must want me with him for some reason.

In these final days, I am surrounded by my family and feel the strength that their love provides.

I told them I'm not leaving. I'm just leading the way.

I'm proud of my family and proud of my accomplishments. Maybe all that work just wore me out, but I enjoyed every minute of it. I've spent my life defying the odds. Now the odds are defying me.

I suppose I can accept the fact that my body can no longer support life, but where does my desire, willpower, creativity, humor, and ingenuity go — those abstract qualities that are the essence of me? Are they part of my soul? Or are they there in my children, passed on like the baton of a relay runner in the race of his life?

GILBERT ORTEGA
April 19, 1936 – September 30, 2003

Afterword

As our Sunday interview sessions continued, I witnessed Gilbert's health failing from the complications of diabetes. Like most people with type 2 diabetes, he didn't understand how it could do so much destruction. I did. I had witnessed the ravages of diabetes when it took my husband's life a few years earlier. For me it was a chilling irony that gave credence to many gut-level conversations with Gilbert about his health.

We talked at length about his dilemma and his prognosis; he was always positive that his inner strength would defy the odds.

But I could see him weakening. He never complained, and he always said he felt fine. Eventually, he admitted that he thought he was on his way out. He was face to face with his own mortality. We talked about death. Our conversations were honest and open.

But he persevered as though he could conquer it like a bump in the business road.

As the Sundays went on, he grew weaker — sometimes he was in his pajamas when I showed up with my tape recorder and my laptop. Even though he didn't have the strength to comb his hair, he was determined to tell his story. Always softspoken, his voice was reduced to nearly a whisper. He said the book was probably the last thing he would accomplish. And it was important to him. He wanted it for his family — almost exclusively.

Soon he got sicker. He was rushed to the hospital, and the prognosis was bleak. He was told there was nothing left to save him. His body was shutting down. Diabetes had siezed its final grip on his existence. He asked his family to take him home. He wanted to die there — not in a hospital. A family vigil ensued. Only close relatives and friends were allowed through the gates.

Cars jammed the long driveway, and the old Navajo wagon under the mesquite tree sank deeper into the earth.

Hopelessness was in the air.

A few days before he died, Gilbert asked for me to come to his bedside. He had some final remarks for the book. "Where is your tape recorder?" he whispered, lifting his head a little. I thought he wouldn't notice that I didn't have it with me this time. I had just brought a pad and a pen because I assumed it would be disrespectful to record him when he was so close to death.

He wanted to talk about dying. "Even though I'm not ready, God must want me for some reason." He seemed to be talking himself into acceptance. "I've spent my life defying the odds. Now the odds are defying me." His remarks about his family were touching and poignant.

I knew I had to muster the courage to say goodbye.

I told him that I felt fortunate having gotten to know the real Gilbert Ortega, and how much respect I had gained for him, how I appreciated his intelligence, creativity, perseverance — and his clever wit.

Then I whispered, "I'm going to miss you, Gilbert."

Patricia Bezunartea

Acknowledgements

The family of Gilbert Ortega would like to thank
the many people who shared in his life
and contributed to his success.
Though some have been mentioned
in this memoir, many more
names could fill the pages.
With God's blessing,
the success will continue.
So will the gratitude.

*From left: London, Renée, Asia, Gilbert Jr., Gilbert III, Cheyenne, Linda, Desirée, Taylor,
D.J., Gayle, Gabriel, Valinda, Shalea, Elijah; 2005.*

In Loving Memory

I am grateful to have shared 48 years with Gilbert. We never stopped loving each other, and even though it didn't work for us to stay married, we shared our lives. I credit Gilbert's sparkling wit and clever sense of humor for keeping me close to him all those years. And, in many ways, I believe we owned each other's hearts, and that's why neither of us ever found true love with anyone else.

Together with our four children, our seven grandchildren and one great grandchild, we all shared lots of love and lots of laughter.

In his final days, other loving members of our large extended family gathered around and shared stories and fond memories and lots of love. We were all with him as he passed on.

Even though I miss Gilbert so very much, I know we will all be together again in heaven. For now, I honor his memory, knowing though he is gone, his love will not go away.

Linda VanderWagen Ortega

From Our Hearts, Dad

It has been a wonderful privilege from God to have been with my Dad for 46 years. Even though he has passed on to "Glory," I still feel his presence strongly, and his stores will continue to represent him. He taught me so much and gave me so much. I always knew I was his little girl. His was the kind of love that made me more open to God's love, too.

This book is the gift of my father's treasured memories — from his heart and soul — to all those who knew him. My Dad's life is God's gift to our family, a gift that we must keep on giving.

How great a blessing you are to us, my Daddy.

— Gayle Dean Ortega

Our Dad was our teacher, our "Rock of Gibraltar." He was a man of great strength, great discipline and great determination — full of wisdom, full of integrity, full of accomplishments.

We know you are in a better place, yet we miss you very much. You will never be forgotten. Your lifelong teachings will remain supreme, guiding us and our own children throughout our lives. We will continuously strive to make you proud. Though you are gone from our sight, you will never be gone from our hearts and minds.

We will not fail you. We love you, Dad.

— Desirée Ortega

My dad's dedication to success was phenomenal. He always said, "Never pray for an easy life, but for the strength to make it through a hard one."

You had a dream; now the dream has you.

Dad, I will miss you forever.

— Gilbert Ortega, Jr.

Papa, I realize that when you spoke there was usually an "underlying message of wisdom" but not always spoken. I'm sure you wondered at times if that message was understood.

I heard much more than the "great words" you spoke, and I believe all the knowledge and wisdom you gave us will resurface when needed to stabilize us and truly become a part of us.

I thank God for giving me a great man like you for a father. I love you so much, Papa.

— F. Renée Ortega

FRIDAY, DECEMBER 12, 1991 B1

THE WALL STREET JOURNAL

MARKETPLACE

Industry Focus: SEC laments loss of independence among auditors — Page B4.

Travel: Custom heli-skiing tours: dive bars and cabin fever — Page B8.

Sports: A woman wrestler pins her success on unique athletic goals — Page B2.

Name Front: Martha Stewart gives directions. We (try to) follow them — Page B10.

(1956-1976)

THE FIRST TWENTY YEARS OF BUSINESS

Apache Tears	Apache Junction, AZ
Red Lake Shopping Ctr	Red Lake, NM
Geronimo	Holbrook, AZ
Indian Village	Lupton, AZ
Coffee Cup	Lupton, AZ
Cubero	Cubero, NM
120 W. Coal	Gallup, NM
201 W. Coal	Gallup, NM
E. Hwy 66	Gallup, NM
Top of the World	Continental Divide, NM
7233 E. Main St	Scottsdale, AZ
Camelback/16th St	Phoenix, AZ
Coronado	Albuquerque, NM
Ortega's Old Town	Santa Fe, NM
Oldest Church, Religious Store	Santa Fe, NM
Towne East	Mesquite, TX
Valley View	Dallas, TX
Greenspoint	Houston, TX
Cameron Trading Post & Tourist Ctr.	Cameron, AZ

1976 - Gilbert sells Chain to Joe Atkinson's Trading Company (included in the agreement is a "Two year covenant not to compete").

1976 - Gilbert begins recording a Country and Western Album

CAN is a word of power
TRY is a word each hour
WON'T is a word of retreat
CAN'T is a word of defeat
OUGHT is a word of duty

WILL is a word of beauty
MIGHT is a word of bereavement
DID is a word of achievement

This is the character of a great man

we proudly call our Father.

We love you Dad.

Gayle, Desiree', Gil Jr., and Renee'

THE FRONT LINES
By Kevin Helliker

Gilbert Ortega Built Up A Business by Turning His Buyers Into Sellers

SCOTTSDALE, ARIZ.

EARLY ONE MORNING in 1958, the telephone woke Gilbert Ortega. His dry-goods grocery store was on fire. He arrived at the site on the Navajo Reservation in time to watch the last of it go up in flames. The store was 30 days old. Mr. Ortega hadn't gotten around to insuring it.

"I lost all I had—and a lot I didn't have," he says, referring to the more than $100,000 in debt the store was carrying.

He vowed not to take what he calls the easy way out: bankruptcy. "That's what everyone told me to do," he says. So how does a 21-year-old with two children climb out of such a deep hole?

He makes an even greater gamble. Mr. Ortega planned to build a bigger business based on his anticipation of a huge growth in one local market: tourism. To meet visitors' demands, he would do an unusual about-face, turning his buyers into sellers. Along the way, he also chased a dream of being a musician.

Mr. Ortega is a descendant of a family of Spanish traders, and grew up on the Navajo Reservation, based in Windowrock, Ariz. In deciding to sell for the Indians instead of to them, he recognized something apparent to few others—not everything of value had been taken from Native Americans. "These people are the best artists in the country," he says.

Before putting his plan into action, Mr. Ortega had to work awhile for other retailers, including his father, to keep up payments on his debt. Though he didn't meet every payment on time, or avoid entirely the litigation from which bankruptcy court would have protected him, his creditors admired his effort.

"He met his obligations, even though it meant he walked rather than drove," recalls Paris Derizotis, a retired state judge in New Mexico and former director of a Gallup, N.M., bank that was one of Mr. Ortega's creditors.

THE APPROACH paid off. Long before he had retired that debt, "those same lenders put me back in business," says Mr. Ortega, who is 60 years old.

In the late 1950s, most Indian arts and crafts shops sold to the few non-Indians interested enough to visit reservations. But Mr. Ortega decided to set up trading posts all along Route 66 and Interstate 40 to cater to the enormous crowds traveling between the East and California. He also introduced a new concept to the Indians: marketing. From Dallas to California, drivers encountered billboards inviting them to shop Gilbert Ortega for Indian arts and crafts.

Although many travelers preferred the experience of buying directly from Indians at fairs or roadside stands, to others Gilbert Ortega offered the perfect combination: shops that were small and quaint but well-known. "Tourists figure a guy with this many stores must be reputable," he says.

Trust is an issue. Items at a Gilbert Ortega store range in price from $25 to $50,000, and tourists trust the store to know the true value of the jewelry or pottery. Authenticity is another issue: As much as half the art sold in the U.S. as Indian-made actually comes from overseas.

It isn't likely many tourists ever heard about Mr. Ortega's determination to make good on the debt on his burned-down store. But his vendors and creditors knew about it, and even a tourism business bene-

E Net Danfold

fits from good word of mouth.

By the late 1970s, Gilbert Ortega stores numbered 16, making him the nation's largest seller of Indian art. His stores brought so much revenue to his disadvantaged vendors, American Indians, that the appreciative governor of New Mexico proclaimed a Gilbert Ortega Day. Arizona's governor honored him similarly.

WITH HIS DEBTS paid off, Mr. Ortega found himself missing the intensity of that drive to redeem himself. He wanted a new challenge. So Mr. Ortega, who played in a country band in high school, sold off his stores and headed to Nashville, Tenn., to cut an album. Two songs—"Is It Wrong?" and "I Don't Believe I'll Fall in Love Today"—broke Billboard magazine's Top 100 country chart.

But the success of his album, "The King of Indian Jewelry Goes Country," confirmed what the "NDN ART" license plate on his Rolls Royce suggests, that his true love is Indian art. On his office walls hang photographs of himself with country stars Tanya Tucker and George Jones, but the names he drops in an interview are those of Indian artists such as Tony Da, Robert Redbird and James Lonewolf.

So he dived back into his former business. Instead of operating across the Southwest, this time he opened stores in one market: metropolitan Phoenix, especially Scottsdale. His strategy? Imagine a mall where one store occupies every other space. From the Gilbert Ortega store that houses his office on Main Street, he looks at a Gilbert Ortega store just opened across the street. It is the fifth Gilbert Ortega store in an area of just a few blocks.

Although 80% of his sales go to tourists walking the streets of historic Scottsdale, he advertises heavily on local buses. These advertisements tend to reach only locals. "But when tourists want to know where to buy Indian art, they ask locals," says Mr. Ortega.

When asked to sum up his advice on how to recover from devastating financial losses or forays into country music, he smiles and offers his motto: "Early to bed, early to rise, work like hell and advertise."

Tom Petzinger is on vacation.

(1978-2003)

GILBERT RETURNS TO HIS FIRST LOVE OF INDIAN ART AND REBUILDS A NEW CHAIN

7215 E. Main St	Scottsdale, AZ
Lincoln Village	Scottsdale, AZ
Hyatt Regency	Phoenix, AZ
Corner, 1st Ave/Brown	Scottsdale, AZ
Indian Village on Main	Scottsdale, AZ
5th Ave, 7155 East	Scottsdale, AZ
Coppermine Hyatt Regency	Phoenix, AZ
Colonnade	Phoenix, AZ
Hilton Village	Scottsdale, AZ
Park Central	Phoenix, AZ
Christown	Phoenix, AZ
Grand Center	Sun City, AZ
Arizona Turquoise/5th Ave	Scottsdale, AZ
Arizona Turquoise II/5th Ave	Scottsdale, AZ
Collectables/5th Ave	Scottsdale, AZ
Main Street, 7229 East	Scottsdale, AZ
G.O. Gallery/ 5th Ave	Scottsdale, AZ
Koshari's/ Borgata	Scottsdale, AZ
Spanish Village	Carefree, AZ
Dominique/ Borgata	Scottsdale, AZ
Von Grabill Gallery	Scottsdale, AZ
Redbird/ Main St	Scottsdale, AZ
Mill Avenue	Tempe, AZ
Lulu Belle's	Scottsdale, AZ
Mi Mundo @ the Galleria	Scottsdale, AZ

GO Gallery
The Rug Room
Shalako
Le Cowboy
Desiree' Eclectic Vogue
Koshari's II

I-17	New River, AZ
Gilbert Ortega Museum	Scottsdale, AZ
Fashion Square	Scottsdale, AZ

A family gathering, 1995, from bottom left: Shalea, Linda, Asia, Gilbert, Gayle,
Top row from left: Valinda, Renée, Desirée and Grace, Linda's mother.

The guys get together: grandson D.J., Gilbert, Gilbert Jr., and Gilbert III.

Growing family, from bottom left:
grandchildren D.J. Stanford, Valinda Sarracino, Shalea Sarracino, Gilbert III
Top left: Desirée, Renée, Asia Ortega-Farrar (granddaughter), Linda, Gayle, Gilbert Jr., Cheyenne.

Gilbert, Linda, Gayle, Robin Sarracino, Grace and Bernie VanderWagen
at Gayle and Robin's wedding – February 17, 1985.

Gilbert and Linda with bride-to-be Renée
January 29, 1989.

Linda and Gilbert celebrate with Desirée when she was selected
Hispanic Business Woman of the Year.

Desirée and Linda with Gilbert at his multi-million dollar art auction
March, 1995.

Gilbert, Jr. shown with his father and with his mother on his wedding day.

Gilbert and granddaughter, Asia, 1995.

Gilbert and granddaughter, Cheyenne, 2002.